To

_____

From

_____

Date

_____

PRAYERS & PROMISES

FOR TEACHERS

Parable
3563 Empleo
St. San Luis Obispo, CA 93401

The quoted ideas expressed in this book (but not Scripture verses) are not, in all cases, exact quotations, as some have been edited for clarity and brevity. In all cases, the author has attempted to maintain the speaker's original intent. In some cases, quoted material for this book was obtained from secondary sources, primarily print media. While every effort was made to ensure the accuracy of these sources, the accuracy cannot be guaranteed. For additions, deletions, corrections, or clarifications in future editions of this text, please write Parable.

The Holy Bible, King James Version

The Holy Bible, New King James Version (NKJV) Copyright © 1982 by Thomas Nelson, Inc. Used by permission.

New Century Version®. (NCV) Copyright © 1987, 1988, 1991 by Word Publishing, a division of Thomas Nelson, Inc. All rights reserved. Used by permission.

International Children's Bible®, New Century Version®. (ICB) Copyright © 1986, 1988, 1999 by Tommy Nelson™, a division of Thomas Nelson, Inc. All rights reserved. Used by permission.

The Holman Christian Standard Bible™ (HCSB) Copyright © 1999, 2000, 2001 by Holman Bible Publishers. Used by permission.

The Holy Bible, New International Version®. (NIV) Copyright © 1973, 1978, 1984 International Bible Society. Used by permission of Zondervan. All rights reserved.

The Holy Bible. New Living Translation (NLT) copyright © 1996 Tyndale Charitable Trust. Used by permission of Tyndale House Publishers.

Scripture taken from The Message. (MSG) Copyright © 1993, 1994, 1995, 1996, 2000, 2001, 2002. Used by permission of NavPress Publishing Group.

The New American Standard Bible®, (NASB) Copyright © 1960, 1962, 1963, 1968, 1971, 1972, 1973, 1975, 1977, 1995 by The Lockman Foundation. Used by permission.

Cover Design by Kim Russell / Wahoo Designs
Page Layout by Bart Dawson

ISBN-13 978-1-58334-441-5

ISBN-10 1-58334-441-1

Printed in the United States of America

PRAYERS
&PROMISES

FOR TEACHERS

Table of Contents

INTRODUCTION

God has given you a book of promises upon which you, as a Christian teacher, can and must depend. That book, of course, is the Holy Bible. The Bible is a priceless gift, a tool that God intends for you to use in every aspect of your life. Yet sometimes, you may be tempted to treat the Bible less like a guidebook and more like a history book—don't make that mistake! Instead, trust God's promises and use His Word as an indispensable guide for life here on earth and for life eternal.

Whether you teach graduate school or Sunday School, whether you lecture at seminary or at Vacation Bible School, you need and deserve a regularly scheduled conference with the ultimate Teacher. After all, you are God's emissary, a person charged with molding lives. God takes your teaching duties very seriously, and so should you.

So, if you are fortunate enough to find yourself in the role of teacher, accept a hearty congratulations and a profound word of thanks. And then, take a few moments to consider the promises on these pages. Remember that God honors your profession just as surely as He offers His loving abundance to you and your students. With God's help, you are destined to reshape eternity. It's a big job, but don't worry: You and God, working together, can handle it.

ABUNDANCE

But this I say, He which soweth sparingly shall reap also sparingly; and he which soweth bountifully shall reap also bountifully.

2 Corinthians 9:6 KJV

My cup runneth over. Surely goodness and mercy shall follow me all the days of my life: and I will dwell in the house of the LORD for ever.

Psalm 23:5-6 KJV

Ask and it will be given to you; seek and you will find; knock and the door will be opened to you. For everyone who asks receives; he who seeks finds; and to him who knocks, the door will be opened.

Matthew 7:7-8 NIV

His master replied, "Well done, good and faithful servant! You have been faithful with a few things; I will put you in charge of many things. Come and share your master's happiness!"

Matthew 25:21 NIV

I am come that they might have life, and that they might have it more abundantly.

John 10:10 KJV

In the 10th chapter of John, when Jesus talks of the abundant life, is He talking about material riches or earthly fame? Hardly. The Son of God came to this world not to give it prosperity, but to give it salvation. Thankfully for Christians, our Savior's abundance is both spiritual and eternal; it never falters—even if we do—and it never dies. We need only to open our hearts to Him, and His grace becomes ours.

God's gifts are available to all, but those gifts are not guaranteed; God's gifts must be claimed by those who choose to follow Christ. As we go about our daily lives, inside the classroom and out, may we accept God's promise of spiritual abundance, and may we share it with a world in desperate need of the Master's healing touch.

God has promised us abundance, peace, and eternal life. These treasures are ours for the asking; all we must do is claim them. One of the great mysteries of life is why on earth do so many of us wait so very long to lay claim to God's gifts?

Marie T. Freeman

Dear Lord, thank You for the abundant life that is mine through Christ Jesus. Give me courage to claim the spiritual riches that You have promised, and lead me according to Your plan for my life, today and always. Amen

ACCEPTANCE

For everything created by God is good, and nothing should be rejected if it is received with thanksgiving.

1 Timothy 4:4 HCSB

Should we accept only good from God and not adversity?

Job 2:10 HCSB

Come to terms with God and be at peace; in this way good will come to you.

Job 22:21 HCSB

Sheathe your sword! Should I not drink the cup that the Father has given Me?

John 18:11 HCSB

A man's heart plans his way, but the Lord determines his steps.

Proverbs 16:9 HCSB

All of us must, from time to time, endure days filled with suffering and pain. And as human beings with limited understanding, we can never fully understand the plans of our Father in heaven. But as believers in a benevolent God, we must always trust Him.

When Jesus went to the Mount of Olives, He poured out His heart to God (Luke 22). Jesus knew of the agony that He was destined to endure, but He also knew that God's will must be done.

We, like our Savior, face trials that bring fear and trembling to the very depths of our souls, but like Christ, we, too, must seek God's will, not our own. When we learn to accept God's will without reservation, we experience the peace that He offers to wise believers who trust Him completely.

———

Dear Lord, let me live in the present, not the past. Let me focus on my blessings, not my sorrows. Give me the wisdom to be thankful for the gifts that I do have, not bitter about the things that I don't have. Let me accept what was, let me give thanks for what is, and let me have faith in what most surely will be: the promise of eternal life with You. Amen

ACTION

Therefore, get your minds ready for action, being self-disciplined, and set your hope completely on the grace to be brought to you at the revelation of Jesus Christ.

1 Peter 1:13 HCSB

But prove yourselves doers of the word, and not merely hearers.

James 1:22 NASB

Are there those among you who are truly wise and understanding? Then they should show it by living right and doing good things with a gentleness that comes from wisdom.

James 3:13 NCV

The prudent see danger and take refuge, but the simple keep going and suffer from it.

Proverbs 27:12 NIV

For the Kingdom of God is not just fancy talk; it is living by God's power.

1 Corinthians 4:20 NLT

The old saying is both familiar and true: actions speak louder than words. And as believers, we must beware: our actions should always give credence to the changes that Christ can make in the lives of those who walk with Him.

God calls upon each of us to act in accordance with His will and with respect for His commandments. If we are to be responsible believers, we must realize that it is never enough simply to hear the instructions of God; we must also live by them. And it is never enough to wait idly by while others do God's work here on earth; we, too, must act. Doing God's work is a responsibility that each of us must bear, and when we do, our loving Heavenly Father rewards our efforts with a bountiful harvest.

Whoever wishes to hold the fortress of contemplation must first of all train in the camp of action.

Pope St. Gregory the Great

Dear Lord, I have heard Your Word, and I have felt Your presence in my heart; let me act accordingly. Let my words and deeds serve as a testimony to the changes You have made in my life. Let me praise You, Father, by following in the footsteps of Your Son, and let others see Him through me. Amen

ADVERSITY

No discipline seems pleasant at the time, but painful. Later on, however, it produces a harvest of righteousness and peace for those who have been trained by it.

Hebrews 12:11 NIV

For though a righteous man falls seven times, he rises again . . . .

Proverbs 24:16 NIV

The Lord lifts the burdens of those bent beneath their loads. The Lord loves the righteous.

Psalm 146:8 NLT

Come to me, all you who are weary and burdened, and I will give you rest. Take my yoke upon you and learn from me, for I am gentle and humble in heart, and you will find rest for your souls. For my yoke is easy and my burden is light.

Matthew 11:28-30 NIV

Be of good cheer; I have overcome the world.

John 16:33 KJV

Teachers of every generation have experienced challenges, and this generation is no different. But, today's teachers face difficulties that previous generations could have scarcely imagined. Thankfully, although the world continues to change, God's love remains constant. And, He remains ready to comfort us and strengthen us whenever we turn to Him.

Because we human beings have the ability to think, we also have the ability to worry. All of us, even the most faithful believers, are plagued by occasional periods of discouragement and doubt. Even though we hold tightly to God's promise of salvation—even though we believe sincerely in God's love and protection—we may find ourselves fretting over the countless details of everyday life.

Where is the best place to take our worries? We should take them to God. We should seek protection from the One who cannot be moved. Then, when we have genuinely turned our concerns over to God, we should worry less and trust Him more, because God is trustworthy, and He is our protector.

———

Dear Lord, when I face the inevitable disappointments of life, give me perspective and faith. When I am discouraged, give me the strength to trust Your promises and follow Your will. And let me live with the assurance that You are firmly in control, and that Your love endures forever. Amen

ANGER

But now you must also put away all the following: anger, wrath, malice, slander, and filthy language from your mouth.

Colossians 3:8 HCSB

Let all bitterness, and wrath, and anger, and clamor, and evil speaking, be put away from you, with all malice: and be ye kind one to another, tender-hearted, forgiving one another, even as God for Christ's sake hath forgiven you.

Ephesians 4:31-32 KJV

But I tell you that men will have to give account on the day of judgment for every careless word they have spoken. For by your words you will be acquitted, and by your words you will be condemned.

Matthew 12:36-37 NIV

A patient man has great understanding, but a quick-tempered man displays folly.

Proverbs 14:29 NIV

Don't let your spirit rush to be angry, for anger abides in the heart of fools.

Ecclesiastes 7:9 HCSB

Teaching, like every job, has its fair share of frustrations—some great and some small. Sometimes, those frustrations may cause you to reach the boiling point. But here's a word of warning: When you're tempted to lose your temper over the minor inconveniences of the teaching profession, don't do it—don't give voice to your angry thoughts.

If you make haste to speak angry words, you will inevitably say things that you'll soon regret. Remember: God will help you control your temper if you ask Him to do so. And the time to ask Him is before your temper gets the best of you—not after.

———

Acrid bitterness inevitably seeps into the lives of people who harbor grudges and suppress anger, and bitterness is always a poison.

Lee Strobel

———

Lord, I can be so impatient, and I can become so angry. Calm me down, Lord, and give me the maturity and the wisdom to be a patient, forgiving teacher. Just as You have forgiven me, Father, let me forgive others so that I can follow the example of Your Son. Amen

ANXIETY

Cast all your anxiety on him because he cares for you.

1 Peter 5:7 NIV

Be anxious for nothing, but in everything by prayer and supplication with thanksgiving let your requests be made known to God.

Philippians 4:6 NASB

Let not your heart be troubled: ye believe in God, believe also in me.

John 14:1 KJV

So don't worry about tomorrow, because tomorrow will have its own worries. Each day has enough trouble of its own.

Matthew 6:34 NCV

When you pass through the waters, I will be with you; and through the rivers, they shall not overflow you. When you walk through the fire, you shall not be burned, nor shall the flame scorch you. For I am the Lord your God, The Holy One of Israel, your Savior.

Isaiah 43:2-3 NKJV

We live in a world that seems to invite panic. Everywhere we turn, or so it seems, we are confronted with disturbing images that seem to cry out. "All is lost." But with God, there is always hope.

God calls us to live above and beyond anxiety. God calls us to live by faith, not by fear. He instructs us to trust Him completely, this day and forever. But sometimes, trusting God is difficult, especially when we become caught up in the incessant demands of an anxious world.

When you feel anxious—and you will—return your thoughts to God's love. Then, take your concerns to Him in prayer and, to the best of your ability, leave them there. Whatever "it" is, God is big enough to handle it. Let Him . . . now!

———

Father, sometimes troubles and distractions preoccupy my thoughts and trouble my soul. When I am anxious, Lord, let me turn my prayers to You. When I am worried, give me faith in You. Let me live courageously, Dear God, knowing that You love me and that You will protect me, today and forever. Amen

ARGUMENTS

But I tell you that men will have to give account on the day of judgment for every careless word they have spoken. For by your words you will be acquitted, and by your words you will be condemned.

Matthew 12:36-37 NIV

And be careful that when you get on each other's nerves you don't snap at each other. Look for the best in each other, and always do your best to bring it out.

1 Thessalonians 5:15 MSG

A hot-tempered man stirs up dissension, but a patient man calms a quarrel.

Proverbs 15:18 NIV

God's servant must not be argumentative, but a gentle listener and a teacher who keeps cool, working firmly but patiently with those who refuse to obey. You never know how or when God might sober them up with a change of heart and a turning to the truth.

2 Timothy 2:24-25 MSG

Arguments are seldom won but often lost. When we engage in petty squabbles, our losses usually outpace our gains. When we acquire the unfortunate habit of habitual bickering, we do harm to our friends, to our families, to our coworkers, and to ourselves.

Time and again, God's Word warns us that most arguments are a monumental waste of time, of energy, and of life. In Titus, we are warned to refrain from "foolish arguments," and with good reason. Such arguments usually do more for the devil than they do for God.

So the next time you're tempted to engage in a silly squabble, whether inside the church or outside it, refrain. When you do, you'll put a smile on God's face, and you'll send the devil packing.

Dear Lord, when I am tempted to be argumentative, keep me calm. When I fall prey to pettiness, restore my sense of perspective. When I am gripped by irrational anger, give me serenity. Let me show my thankfulness to You by offering forgiveness to others. And, when I do, may others see Your love reflected through my words and my deeds. Amen

ASKING GOD

What father among you, if his son asks for a fish, will, instead of a fish, give him a snake? Or if he asks for an egg, will give him a scorpion? If you then, who are evil, know how to give good gifts to your children, how much more will the heavenly Father give the Holy Spirit to those who ask Him?

Luke 11:11-13 HCSB

And in that day you will ask Me nothing. Most assuredly, I say to you, whatever you ask the Father in My name He will give you. Until now you have asked nothing in My name. Ask, and you will receive, that your joy may be full.

John 16:23-24 NKJV

Don't worry about anything, but in everything, through prayer and petition with thanksgiving, let your requests be made known to God.

Philippians 4:6 HCSB

So I say to you, keep asking, and it will be given to you. Keep searching, and you will find. Keep knocking, and the door will be opened to you.

Luke 11:9 HCSB

How often do you ask for God's help? Occasionally? Intermittently? Whenever you experience a crisis? Hopefully not. Hopefully, you have developed the habit of asking for God's assistance early and often. And hopefully, you have learned to seek His guidance in every aspect of your life.

God has promised that when you ask for His help, He will not withhold it. So ask. Ask Him to meet the needs of your day. Ask Him for wisdom. Ask Him to lead you, to protect you, and to correct you. And trust the answers He gives.

God stands at the door and waits. When you knock on His door, He answers. Your task, of course, is to seek His guidance prayerfully, confidently, and often.

It is our part to seek, His to grant what we ask; our part to make a beginning, His to bring it to completion; our part to offer what we can, His to finish what we cannot.

St. Jerome

Lord, when I have questions or fears, let me turn to You. When I am weak, let me seek Your strength. When I am discouraged, Father, keep me mindful of Your love and Your grace. In all things, let me seek Your will and Your way, Dear Lord, today and forever. Amen

ATTITUDE

Make your own attitude that of Christ Jesus.

Philippians 2:5 HCSB

Finally brothers, whatever is true, whatever is honorable, whatever is just, whatever is pure, whatever is lovely, whatever is commendable—if there is any moral excellence and if there is any praise—dwell on these things.

Philippians 4:8 HCSB

Set your minds on what is above, not on what is on the earth.

Colossians 3:2 HCSB

A cheerful heart has a continual feast.

Proverbs 15:15 HCSB

For the word of God is living and effective and sharper than any two-edged sword, penetrating as far as to divide soul, spirit, joints, and marrow; it is a judge of the ideas and thoughts of the heart.

Hebrews 4:12 HCSB

As the leader of your classroom, you must beware: your attitudes are contagious. If you're upbeat and optimistic, your students will tend to emulate you. But, if you fall prey to cynicism or pessimism, many of your students will, too. How will you direct your thoughts today? Will you obey the words of Philippians 4:8 by dwelling upon those things that are pure, lovely, and admirable? Or will you allow your thoughts to be hijacked by the negativity that seems to dominate our troubled world.

God intends that you experience joy and abundance, but He will not force His joy upon you; you must claim it for yourself. So, today and every day hereafter, focus your thoughts and your energies upon "things that are excellent and worthy of praise." When you celebrate life, you'll soon discover that many of your students will join in the celebration.

Dear Lord, let me live my life and love my students with a spirit of optimism and hope. Whatever circumstances I face, whether good or bad, triumphal or tragic, may my response reflect a God-honoring, Christ-like attitude of faith and love for You. Amen

BEHAVIOR

Even a child is known by his actions, by whether his conduct is pure and right.

Proverbs 20:11 NIV

Therefore by their fruits you will know them.

Matthew 7:20 NKJV

He who has My commandments and keeps them, it is he who loves Me. And he who loves Me will be loved by My Father, and I will love him and manifest Myself to him.

John 14:21 NKJV

Who is wise and understanding among you? Let him show by good conduct that his works are done in the meekness of wisdom.

James 3:13 NKJV

Light shines on the godly, and joy on those who do right. May all who are godly be happy in the Lord and praise his holy name.

Psalm 97:11-12 NLT

L ife is a series of decisions and choices. Each day, we make countless decisions that can bring us closer to God . . . or not. When we live according to God's commandments, we earn for ourselves the abundance and peace that He intends for our lives. But, when we turn our backs upon God by disobeying Him, we bring needless suffering upon ourselves and our families.

Do you seek God's peace and His blessings? Then obey Him. When you're faced with a difficult choice or a powerful temptation, seek God's counsel and trust the counsel He gives. Invite God into your heart and live according to His commandments. When you do, you will be blessed today, and tomorrow, and forever.

Although God causes all things to work together for good for His children, He still holds us accountable for our behavior.

Kay Arthur

Dear Lord, guide me away from the temptations and distractions of this world, and make me a champion of the faith. Today I will honor You with my thoughts, my actions, and my prayers. I will worship You, Father, with gratitude in my heart and praise on my lips, this day and forever. Amen

CELEBRATION

David and the whole house of Israel were celebrating with all their might before the LORD, with songs and with harps, lyres, tambourines, sistrums and cymbals.

2 Samuel 6:5 NIV

This is the day which the LORD has made; let us rejoice and be glad in it.

Psalm 118:24 NASB

At the dedication of the wall of Jerusalem, the Levites were sought out from where they lived and were brought to Jerusalem to celebrate joyfully the dedication with songs of thanksgiving and with the music of cymbals, harps and lyres.

Nehemiah 12:27 NIV

A happy heart is like a continual feast.

Proverbs 15:15 NCV

Celebrate God all day, every day. I mean, revel in him!

Philippians 4:4 MSG

Are you a teacher who celebrates life? Hopefully you are! God has richly blessed you, and He wants you to rejoice in His gifts.

The 118th Psalm reminds us that today, like every other day, is a cause for celebration. God gives us this day; He fills it to the brim with possibilities, and He challenges us to use it for His purposes. Today is a non-renewable resource—once it's gone, it's gone forever. Our responsibility—as Christians and as teachers—is to use this day in the service of God's will as we share His wisdom and His love.

Some of us seem so anxious about avoiding hell that we forget to celebrate our journey toward heaven.

Philip Yancey

Dear Lord, You have given me so many reasons to celebrate. Today, let me choose an attitude of cheerfulness. Let me be a joyful Christian, Lord, quick to laugh and slow to anger. And, let me share Your goodness with my family, my friends, my neighbors, and my students, this day and every day. Amen

CHARACTER

A good name is more desirable than great riches; to be esteemed is better than silver or gold.

Proverbs 22:1 NIV

In all things showing yourself to be a pattern of good works; in doctrine showing integrity, reverence, incorruptibility . . . .

Titus 2:7 NKJV

As in water face reflects face, so the heart of man reflects man.

Proverbs 27:19 NASB

Not only so, but we also rejoice in our sufferings, because we know that suffering produces perseverance; perseverance, character; and character, hope.

Romans 5:3-4 NIV

The man of integrity walks securely, but he who takes crooked paths will be found out.

Proverbs 10:9 NIV

Wise teachers understand the importance of character . . . and teach it. Character is built slowly over a lifetime. It is the sum of every right decision, every honest word, every noble thought, and every heartfelt prayer. It is forged on the anvil of honorable work and polished by the twin virtues of generosity and humility. Character is a precious thing—difficult to build, but easy to tear down; godly teachers value it and protect it at all costs . . . and they encourage their students to do the same.

———

Character is what you are in the dark.

D. L. Moody

———

Heavenly Father, Your Word instructs me to walk in righteousness and in truth. Make me Your worthy servant, Lord. Let my words be true, and let my actions lead others to You. Amen

CHEERFULNESS

The cheerful heart has a continual feast.

Proverbs 15:15 NIV

A cheerful look brings joy to the heart, and good news gives health to the bones.

Proverbs 15:30 NIV

God loves a cheerful giver.

2 Corinthians 9:7 NIV

Jacob said, "For what a relief it is to see your friendly smile. It is like seeing the smile of God!"

Genesis 33:10 NLT

A cheerful heart is good medicine . . . .

Proverbs 17:22 NIV

Oswald Chambers correctly observed, "Joy is the great note all throughout the Bible." He might have added that joy should also be the cornerstone of learning. Today, let us celebrate life as God intended. Today, let us put smiles on our faces, kind words on our lips, and songs in our hearts. And, while we're at it, let's infuse as much joy as we can into the classroom. God loves a cheerful giver and a cheerful teacher.

Cheerfulness prepares a glorious mind for all the noblest acts of religion—love, adoration, praise, and every union with our God.

St. Elizabeth Ann Seton

Make me a cheerful teacher, Lord. Let me celebrate the day that You have given me, and let me celebrate Your Son. Let me speak words of encouragement and hope to all who cross my path, and let others see the joy and thanksgiving that I feel in my heart for Your priceless gift to the world: Christ Jesus. Amen

CHRIST

The next day John seeth Jesus coming unto him, and saith, Behold the Lamb of God, which taketh away the sin of the world.

John 1:29 KJV

I am the Vine, you are the branches. When you're joined with me and I with you, the relation intimate and organic, the harvest is sure to be abundant.

John 15:5 MSG

To this end was I born, and for this cause came I into the world, that I should bear witness unto the truth.

John 18:37 KJV

For the Son of man is come to save that which was lost.

Matthew 18:11 KJV

Therefore if any man be in Christ, he is a new creature: old things are passed away; behold, all things are become new.

2 Corinthians 5:17 KJV

Hannah Whitall Smith spoke to believers of every generation when she advised, "Keep your face upturned to Christ as the flowers do to the sun. Look, and your soul shall live and grow." How true. When we turn our hearts to Jesus, we receive His blessings, His peace, and His grace.

Christ is the ultimate Savior of mankind and the personal Savior of those who believe in Him. As His servants, we should place Him at the very center of our lives. And, every day that God gives us breath, we should share Christ's love and His message with a world that needs both.

We shall find in Christ enough of everything we need—for the body, for the mind, and for the spirit—to do what He wants us to do as long as He wants us to do it.

Vance Havner

Dear Lord, thank You for the gift of Your Son Jesus, my personal Savior. Let me be a worthy servant of Christ, and let me be ever grateful for His love. Let me always praise You, Lord, as I give thanks for Your Son Jesus and for Your everlasting love. Amen

CHRIST'S LOVE

I am the good shepherd. The good shepherd lays down his life for the sheep.

John 10:11 NIV

But God demonstrates His own love toward us, in that while we were still sinners, Christ died for us.

Romans 5:8 NKJV

As the Father hath loved me, so have I loved you; continue ye in my love.

John 15:9 KJV

Who shall separate us from the love of Christ? Shall tribulation, or distress, or persecution, or famine, or nakedness, or peril, or sword? . . . Yet in all these things we are more than conquerors through Him who loved us.

Romans 8:35,37 NKJV

And I am convinced that nothing can ever separate us from his love. Whether we are high above the sky or in the deepest ocean, nothing in all creation will ever be able to separate us from the love of God that is revealed in Christ Jesus our Lord.

Romans 8:38–39 NLT

How much does Christ love us? More than we, as mere mortals, can comprehend. His love is perfect and steadfast. Even though we are fallible and wayward, the Good Shepherd cares for us still. Even though we have fallen far short of the Father's commandments, Christ loves us with a power and depth that is beyond our understanding. The sacrifice that Jesus made upon the cross was made for each of us, and His love endures to the edge of eternity and beyond.

Christ's love changes everything. When you accept His gift of grace, you are transformed, not only for today, but also for all eternity. If you haven't already done so, accept Jesus Christ as your Savior. He's waiting patiently for you to invite Him into your heart. Please don't make Him wait a single minute longer.

Dear Jesus, You are my Savior and my protector. Give me the courage to trust You completely. Today, I will praise You, I will honor You, and I will live according to Your commandments, so that through me, others might come to know Your perfect love. Amen

CONSCIENCE

Let us draw near to God with a sincere heart in full assurance of faith, having our hearts sprinkled to cleanse us from a guilty conscience and having our bodies washed with pure water.

Hebrews 10:22 NIV

I will maintain my righteousness and never let go of it; my conscience will not reproach me as long as I live.

Job 27:6 NIV

Do not conform any longer to the pattern of this world, but be transformed by the renewing of your mind. Then you will be able to test and approve what God's will is—his good, pleasing and perfect will.

Romans 12:2 NIV

Create in me a pure heart, O God, and renew a steadfast spirit within me.

Psalm 51:10 NIV

So I strive always to keep my conscience clear before God and man.

Acts 24:16 NIV

Simply put, a guilty conscience has the power to torment us. And thankfully, the opposite is also true. Few things in life provide more contentment than a clear conscience—a clear conscience that results from the knowledge that we are obeying God's commandments.

Thoughtful teachers (like you) understand the importance of wise choices and the rewards of a clear conscience . . . and thoughtful teachers (like you) share that message with their students.

To go against one's conscience is neither safe nor right. Here I stand. I cannot do otherwise.

Martin Luther

Dear Lord, You speak to me through the Bible, through the words of others, and through that still, small voice within. Through my conscience, You reveal Your will for my life. Show me Your plan for this day, Heavenly Father, and let me share the Good News of Your Son. Amen

CONTENTMENT

Keep your lives free from the love of money and be content with what you have, because God has said, "Never will I leave you; never will I forsake you."

Hebrews 13:5 NIV

I know what it is to be in need, and I know what it is to have plenty. I have learned the secret of being content in any and every situation, whether well fed or hungry, whether living in plenty or in want. I can do everything through him who gives me strength.

Philippians 4:12-13 NIV

Satisfy us in the morning with your unfailing love, that we may sing for joy and be glad all our days.

Psalm 90:14 NIV

I have learned, in whatsoever state I am, therewith to be content.

Philippians 4:11 KJV

But godliness with contentment is great gain. For we brought nothing into the world, and we can take nothing out of it. But if we have food and clothing, we will be content with that.

1 Timothy 6:6-8 NIV

The world readily offers us many things, but lasting contentment is not one of them. Genuine contentment cannot be found in material possessions, earthly power, human relationships, or transitory fame. Genuine contentment starts with God and His only begotten Son . . . and ends there.

Do you seek the contentment and peace that only God can offer? Then welcome His Son into your heart. Allow Christ to rule over every aspect of your day: talk with Him; walk with Him; be with Him; praise Him. When you do, you will discover the peace and contentment that only God can give.

———

Contentment is trusting God even when things seem out of control.

Charles Stanley

———

Father, show me how to be ambitious in Your work. Let me strive to do Your will here on earth, and as I do, let me find contentment and balance. Let me live in the light of Your will and Your priorities for my life, and when I have done my best, Lord, give me the wisdom to place my faith and my trust in You. Amen

COURAGE

So do not fear, for I am with you; do not be dismayed, for I am your God. I will strengthen you and help you; I will uphold you with my righteous right hand.

Isaiah 41:10 NIV

Peace I leave with you, my peace I give unto you: not as the world giveth, give I unto you. Let not your heart be troubled, neither let it be afraid.

John 14:27 KJV

In thee, O Lord, do I put my trust; let me never be put into confusion.

Psalm 71:1 KJV

I can do everything through him that gives me strength.

Philippians 4:13 NIV

The LORD himself goes before you and will be with you; he will never leave you nor forsake you. Do not be afraid; do not be discouraged.

Deuteronomy 31:8 NIV

A storm rose quickly on the Sea of Galilee, and the disciples were afraid. Although they had seen Jesus perform many miracles, the disciples feared for their lives, so they turned to their Savior, and He calmed the waters and the wind.

Sometimes, we, like the disciples, feel threatened by the inevitable storms of life. And when we are fearful, we, too, can turn to Christ for courage and for comfort.

The next time you're afraid, remember that the One who calmed the wind and the waves is also your personal Savior. And remember that the ultimate battle has already been won at Calvary. We, as believers, can live courageously in the promises of our Lord . . . and we should.

———

Courage is almost a contradiction in terms. It means a strong desire to live taking the form of a readiness to die.

G. K. Chesterton

———

Lord, at times, this world is a fearful place. At times, I fear for my family and for my students. Yet, You have promised that You are with me always. With You as my protector, I am not afraid. Today, Dear Lord, let me live courageously as I place my trust in You. Amen

DECISIONS

But Daniel purposed in his heart that he would not defile himself . . . .

Daniel 1:8 KJV

I am offering you life or death, blessings or curses. Now, choose life! . . . To choose life is to love the Lord your God, obey him, and stay close to him.

Deuteronomy 30:19-20 NCV

The thing you should want most is God's kingdom and doing what God wants. Then all these other things you need will be given to you.

Matthew 6:33 NCV

If you don't know what you're doing, pray to the Father. He loves to help. You'll get his help, and won't be condescended to when you ask for it. Ask boldly, believingly, without a second thought. People who "worry their prayers" are like wind-whipped waves. Don't think you're going to get anything from the Master that way, adrift at sea, keeping all your options open.

James 1:5-8 MSG

Are you facing a difficult decision, a troubling circumstance, or a powerful temptation? If so, it's time to step back, to stop focusing on what "the world" wants you to do, and to focus, instead, on what your conscience tells you to do. The world will often lead you astray, but your conscience will not.

Life is an exercise in decision-making. Today and every day you must make choices: choices about what you will do, what you will worship, and how you will think. When in doubt, make choices that you sincerely believe will bring you to a closer relationship with God. And if you're uncertain of your next step, slow yourself down long enough to pray about it. When you do, answers will come. And you may rest assured that when God answers prayer, His answers are the right ones for you.

———

Lord, help me to make decisions that are pleasing to You. Help me to be honest, patient, thoughtful, and obedient. And above all, help me to follow the teachings of Jesus, not just today, but every day. Amen

DISCIPLINE

Folly is loud; she is undisciplined and without knowledge.

Proverbs 9:13 NIV

Whoever gives heed to instruction prospers, and blessed is he that trusts in the Lord.

Proverbs 16:20 NIV

My son, do not make light of the Lord's discipline, and do not lose heart when he rebukes you, because the Lord disciplines those he loves, and he punishes everyone he accepts as a son.

Hebrews 12:5 NIV

No discipline seems pleasant at the time, but painful. Later on, however, it produces a harvest of righteousness and peace for those who have been trained by it.

Hebrews 12:11 NIV

He who heeds discipline shows the way to life, but whoever ignores correction leads others astray.

Proverbs 10:17 NIV

As leaders of the classroom, we are charged with teaching discipline and, on occasion, dispensing it. We do so in the hopes that our students will learn that disciplined behavior is at the very foundation of successful living.

Those who study the Bible are confronted again and again with God's intention that His children (of all ages) lead disciplined lives. God doesn't reward laziness or misbehavior. To the contrary, He expects His own to adopt a disciplined approach to their lives, and He punishes those who disobey His commandments.

Wise teachers demonstrate the importance of discipline by their words and by their actions. Wise students pay attention . . . and learn.

———

The alternative to discipline is disaster.

Vance Havner

———

Heavenly Father, make me a teacher of discipline and righteousness, and make me a diligent teacher in the service of Your Son, Christ Jesus. Let me teach others by the faithfulness of my conduct, and let me follow Your will and Your Word, today and every day. Amen

DREAMS

I came so they can have real and eternal life, more and better life than they ever dreamed of.

John 10:10 MSG

It is pleasant to see dreams come true, but fools will not turn from evil to attain them.

Proverbs 13:19 NLT

Where there is no vision, the people perish . . . .

Proverbs 29:18 KJV

I can do everything through him that gives me strength.

Philippians 4:13 NIV

Live full lives, full in the fullness of God. God can do anything, you know—far more than you could ever imagine or guess or request in your wildest dreams! He does it not by pushing us around but by working within us, his Spirit deeply and gently within us.

Ephesians 3:19-20 MSG

Are you willing to entertain the possibility that God has big plans in store for you as well as your students? Hopefully so. Yet sometimes, especially if you've recently experienced a life-altering disappointment, you may find it difficult to envision the possibility of a brighter future. If so, it's time to stop placing limitations upon yourself, upon your students, and upon God.

Your Heavenly Father created you with unique gifts and untapped talents; your job is to tap them. When you do, you'll begin to feel an increasing sense of confidence in yourself and in your future. Then, you can share that confidence with your students, with your family, and with your friends.

It takes courage to dream big dreams. You will discover that courage when you do three things: accept the past, trust God to handle the future, and make the most of the time He has given you today.

Nothing is too difficult for God, and no dreams are too big for Him—not even yours. So start living—and dreaming—accordingly.

Dear Lord, give me the courage to dream and the wisdom to help my students do likewise. When I am worried or weary, give me strength for today and hope for tomorrow. Keep me mindful of Your miraculous power, Your infinite love, and Your eternal salvation. Amen

God's Promises About . . .

ENCOURAGEMENT

Watch the way you talk. Let nothing foul or dirty come out of your mouth. Say only what helps, each word a gift.

Ephesians 4:29 MSG

Encourage each other. Live in harmony and peace. Then the God of love and peace will be with you.

2 Corinthians 13:11 NLT

Let the word of Christ dwell in you richly in all wisdom; teaching and admonishing one another in psalms and hymns and spiritual songs, singing with grace in your hearts to the Lord.

Colossians 3:16 KJV

But encourage one another day after day, as long as it is still called "Today," so that none of you will be hardened by the deceitfulness of sin.

Hebrews 3:13 NASB

Let's see how inventive we can be in encouraging love and helping out, not avoiding worshipping together as some do but spurring each other on.

Hebrews 10:24-25 MSG

For young people experiencing life-here-in-the-new-millennium, the world can be a difficult and uncertain place. Many of our students are in desperate need of a smile or an encouraging word, and since we don't always know who needs our help, the best strategy is to encourage all those who cross our paths.

Great teachers encourage impressionable students to believe in themselves. Great teachers inspire confidence. Great teachers encourage their students to learn, to work, to grow, and to persevere.

So, as you make plans for the upcoming day, promise yourself that you'll be the kind of teacher who encourages students to believe in themselves. Never has the need been greater.

———

Do you wonder where you can go for encouragement and motivation? Run to Jesus.

Max Lucado

———

Dear Father, make me an encouraging teacher. Just as You have lifted me up, let me also lift up my students in the spirit of encouragement and hope. Today, let me help my students find the strength and the courage to use their gifts according to Your master plan. Amen

God's Promises About . . .

ENERGY

Those who hope in the LORD will renew their strength. They will soar on wings like eagles; they will run and not grow weary, they will walk and not be faint.

Isaiah 40:31 NIV

The plans of the diligent lead to profit.

Proverbs 21:5 NIV

He did it with all his heart, and prospered.

2 Chronicles 31:21 KJV

And whatsoever ye do, do it heartily.

Colossians 3:23 KJV

Never be lacking in zeal, but keep your spiritual fervor, serving the Lord.

Romans 12:11 NIV

All of us have moments when we feel drained. All of us suffer through difficult days, trying times, and perplexing periods of our lives. Thankfully, God stands ready and willing to give us comfort and strength if we turn to Him.

Burning the candle at both ends is tempting but potentially destructive. Instead, we should place first things first by saying no to the things that we simply don't have the time or the energy to do. As we establish our priorities, we should turn to God and to His Holy Word for guidance.

God does not dispense strength and encouragement like a druggist fills your prescription. The Lord doesn't promise to give us something to take so we can handle our weary moments. He promises us Himself. That is all. And that is enough.

Charles Swindoll

Lord, let me find my strength in You. When I am weary, give me rest. When I feel overwhelmed, let me look to You for my priorities. Let Your power be my power, Lord, and let Your way be my way, today and forever. Amen

ENTHUSIASM

Never be lazy in your work, but serve the Lord enthusiastically.

Romans 12:11 NLT

Whatever work you do, do your best, because you are going to the grave, where there is no working . . . .

Ecclesiastes 9:10 NCV

I have seen that there is nothing better than for a person to enjoy his activities, because that is his reward. For who can enable him to see what will happen after he dies?

Ecclesiastes 3:22 HCSB

Do your work with enthusiasm. Work as if you were serving the Lord, not as if you were serving only men and women.

Ephesians 6:7 NCV

Whatever you do, do it enthusiastically, as something done for the Lord and not for men.

Colossians 3:23 HCSB

Norman Vincent Peale advised, "Get absolutely enthralled with something. Throw yourself into it with abandon. Get out of yourself. Be somebody. Do something." His words still ring true, especially in the classroom. But sometimes, when the stresses of everyday life seem overwhelming, you may not feel very enthusiastic about yourself or your students.

If you're a teacher with too many obligations and too few hours in which to meet them, you are not alone. Teaching can be a demanding profession. But don't fret. Instead, focus upon God and upon His love for you. Then, ask Him for the strength you need to fulfill your responsibilities. God will give you the enthusiasm to do the most important things on today's to-do list . . . if you ask Him. So ask Him. Now.

Your enthusiasm will be infectious, stimulating, and attractive to others. They will love you for it. They will go for you and with you.

Norman Vincent Peale

Lord, when the classroom leaves me exhausted, let me turn to You for strength and for renewal. When I follow Your will for my life, You will renew my enthusiasm. Let Your will be my will, Lord, and let me find my strength in You. Amen

ETERNAL LIFE

And this is the testimony: God has given us eternal life, and this life is in His Son. The one who has the Son has life. The one who doesn't have the Son of God does not have life.

1 John 5:11-12 HCSB

Pursue righteousness, godliness, faith, love, endurance, and gentleness. Fight the good fight for the faith; take hold of eternal life, to which you were called and have made a good confession before many witnesses.

1 Timothy 6:11-12 HCSB

Jesus said to her, "I am the resurrection and the life. The one who believes in Me, even if he dies, will live. Everyone who lives and believes in Me will never die—ever. Do you believe this?"

John 11:25-26 HCSB

For God loved the world in this way: He gave His only Son, so that everyone who believes in Him will not perish but have eternal life.

John 3:16 HCSB

Your ability to envision the future, like your life here on earth, is limited. God's vision, however, is not burdened by any such limitations. He sees all things, He knows all things, and His plans for you endure for all time.

God's plans are not limited to the events of life-here-on-earth. Your Heavenly Father has bigger things in mind for you . . . much bigger things. So praise the Creator for the gift of eternal life and share the Good News with all who cross your path. You have given your heart to the Son, so you belong to the Father—today, tomorrow, and for all eternity.

I can still hardly believe it. I, with shriveled, bent fingers, atrophied muscles, gnarled knees, and no feeling from the shoulders down, will one day have a new body—light, bright and clothed in righteousness—powerful and dazzling.

Joni Eareckson Tada

I know, Lord, that this world is not my home; I am only here for a brief while. And, You have given me the priceless gift of eternal life through Your Son Jesus. Keep the hope of heaven fresh in my heart, and, while I am in this world, help me to pass through it with faith in my heart and praise on my lips, for You. Amen

EXAMPLE

Do everything without grumbling and arguing, so that you may be blameless and pure.

Philippians 2:14–15 HCSB

Set an example of good works yourself, with integrity and dignity in your teaching.

Titus 2:7 HCSB

For the kingdom of God is not in talk but in power.

1 Corinthians 4:20 HCSB

Therefore since we also have such a large cloud of witnesses surrounding us, let us lay aside every weight and the sin that so easily ensnares us, and run with endurance the race that lies before us.

Hebrews 12:1 HCSB

You should be an example to the believers in speech, in conduct, in love, in faith, in purity.

1 Timothy 4:12 HCSB

We teach our students by the words we speak and the lives we lead, but not necessarily in that order. Sometimes, our actions speak so loudly that they drown out our words completely. That's why, as teachers, we must make certain that the lives we lead are in harmony with the lessons we preach.

Are you the kind of teacher whose life serves as a memorable model of righteousness and godliness? If so, you are a powerful force for good in your classroom and in your world.

Phillips Brooks advised, "Be such a man, and live such a life, that if every man were such as you, and every life a life like yours, this earth would be God's Paradise." And that's sound advice because our families and our students are watching . . . and so, for that matter, is God.

It is a wonderful thing for an upright man who cannot teach others by precept to teach them by the piety of his conduct.

Cassiodorus

Dear Lord, because I am a teacher, I am an example to my students. Let me be a worthy example, Father, so that my words and my deeds may be a tribute to You. Amen

FAITH

Now faith is being sure of what we hope for and certain of what we do not see.

Hebrews 11:1 NIV

But without faith it is impossible to please him: for he that cometh to God must believe that he is, and that he is a rewarder of them that diligently seek him.

Hebrews 11:6 KJV

Faith without works is dead . . . .

James 2:20 KJV

Anything is possible if you have faith.

Mark 9:23 TLB

Have faith in the LORD your God and you will be upheld.

2 Chronicles 20:20 NIV

As a dedicated member of the teaching profession, you have mountains to climb and mountains to move. Jesus taught His disciples that if they had faith, they could move mountains. You can too. When you place your faith, your trust, indeed your life in the hands of Christ Jesus, you'll be amazed at the marvelous things He can do.

When a suffering woman sought healing by simply touching the hem of His garment, Jesus turned and said, "Daughter, be of good comfort; thy faith hath made thee whole" (Matthew 9:22 KJV). We, too, can be made whole when we place our faith completely and unwaveringly in the person of Jesus Christ.

So, if your faith is being tested, know that your Savior is near. If you reach out to Him in faith, He will give you peace, perspective, and hope. If you are content to touch even the smallest fragment of the Master's garment, He will make you whole.

———

Dear Lord, help me to be a teacher whose faith is strong and whose heart is pure. Help me to remember that You are always near and that You can overcome any challenge. With Your love and Your power, Lord, I can live courageously and faithfully today and every day. Amen

FORGIVENESS

If you forgive those who sin against you, your heavenly Father will forgive you. But if you refuse to forgive others, your Father will not forgive your sins.

Matthew 6:14-15 NLT

And be ye kind one to another, tenderhearted, forgiving one another, even as God for Christ's sake hath forgiven you.

Ephesians 4:32 KJV

Whenever you stand praying, forgive, if you have anything against anyone, so that your Father in heaven will also forgive you your transgressions.

Mark 11:25 NASB

Praise the Lord, I tell myself, and never forget the good things he does for me. He forgives all my sins and heals all my diseases.

Psalm 103:3 NLT

Have mercy on me, O God, according to your unfailing love; according to your great compassion blot out my transgressions. Wash away all my iniquity and cleanse me from my sin.

Psalm 51:1-2 NIV

Even the most mild-mannered teachers will, on occasion, have reason to become angry with the inevitable shortcomings of students. But wise teachers are quick to forgive others, just as God has forgiven them.

Teachers, having been placed in positions of leadership, serve as important role models to their students. As such, teachers must be models of forgiveness, both inside the classroom and out.

Are you easily frustrated by the inevitable shortcomings of others? Are you a prisoner of bitterness or regret? If so, perhaps you need a refresher course in the art of forgiveness.

So, if there exists even one person, alive or dead, whom you have not forgiven (and that includes yourself), follow God's commandment and His will for your life: forgive. Hatred and bitterness and regret are not part of God's plan for your life. Forgiveness is.

———

Lord, just as You have forgiven me, I am going to forgive others. When I forgive others, I not only obey Your commandments, but I also free myself from bitterness and regret. Forgiveness is Your way, Lord, and I will make it my way, too. Amen

FUTURE

*"I say this because I know what I am planning for you," says the
Lord. "I have good plans for you, not plans to hurt you. I will give
you hope and a good future."*

Jeremiah 29:11 NCV

*When troubles come and all these awful things happen to you,
in future days you will come back to God, your God, and
listen obediently to what he says. God, your God, is above all a
compassionate God. In the end he will not abandon you, he won't
bring you to ruin, he won't forget the covenant with your ancestors
which he swore to them.*

Deuteronomy 4:30-31 MSG

*Do not boast about tomorrow, for you do not know what a day
may bring forth.*

Proverbs 27:1 NKJV

*What a God we have! And how fortunate we are to have him, this
Father of our Master Jesus! Because Jesus was raised from the dead,
we've been given a brand-new life and have everything to live for,
including a future in heaven—and the future starts now!*

1 Peter 1:3-4 MSG

I n these uncertain times, it's easy to lose hope for the future ... but it's wrong. God instructs us to trust His wisdom, His plan, and His love. When we do so, the future becomes a glorious opportunity to help others, to praise our Creator, and to share God's Good News.

Do you have faith in the ultimate goodness of God's plan? You should. And, do you have faith in the abundant opportunities that await your students? Hopefully, you do. After all, the confidence that you display in your students can be contagious: Your belief in them can have a profound impact on the way they view themselves and their world.

Today, as you stand before your classroom, help your students face the future with optimism, hope, and self-confidence. After all, even in these uncertain times, God still has the last word. And His love endures to all generations, including this one.

———

Lord, sometimes when I think about the future, I worry. Today, I will do a better job of trusting You. If I become discouraged, I will turn to You. If I am afraid, I will seek strength in You. You are my Father, and I will place my hope, my trust, and my faith in You. Amen

God's Promises About . . .

GENEROSITY

Above all, love each other deeply, because love covers a multitude of sins.

1 Peter 4:8 NIV

The man with two tunics should share with him who has none, and the one who has food should do the same.

Luke 3:11 NIV

I tell you the truth, whatever you did for one of the least of these brothers of mine, you did for me.

Matthew 25:40 NIV

The good person is generous and lends lavishly . . . .

Psalm 112:5 MSG

So let him give; not grudgingly, or of necessity: for God loveth a cheerful giver.

2 Corinthians 9:7 KJV

Kindness and generosity are woven into the fabric of the Christian faith. And, because we are important role models to our students, we have an obligation to demonstrate generosity not only by our words, but also by our deeds.

The words of Matthew 10:8 are clear: because we have received so much from our Creator, we are commanded to give freely to His children. As followers of Christ, we have been immeasurably blessed. In return, we must give generously of our time, our possessions, our testimonies, and our love.

Today and every day, let Christ's words be your guide and let His eternal love fill your heart. When you do, your stewardship will be a reflection of your love for Him, and that's exactly as it should be. After all, He loved you first.

Dear Lord, You have been so generous with me; let me be generous with others. Help me to be generous with my time and my possessions as I care for those in need. Help me to teach my students to be cheerful givers, Father, and make us all humble givers, so that the glory and the praise might be Yours. Amen

GIFTS

Now there are varieties of gifts, but the same Spirit. And there are varieties of ministries, and the same Lord.

1 Corinthians 12:4-5 NASB

Do not neglect the spiritual gift that is within you . . . .

1 Timothy 4:14 NASB

Since we have gifts that differ according to the grace given to us, let each exercise them accordingly: if prophecy, according to the proportion of his faith; if service, in his serving; or he who teaches, in his teaching; or he who exhorts, in his exhortation; he who gives, with liberality; he who leads, with diligence; he who shows mercy, with cheerfulness.

Romans 12:6-8 NASB

Every good gift and every perfect gift is from above and comes down from the Father of lights.

James 1:17 NKJV

God has given gifts to each of you from his great variety of spiritual gifts. Manage them well so that God's generosity can flow through you.

1 Peter 4:10 NLT

Perhaps you are one of those lucky teachers who has a natural gift for leading a class. But, even if you have the oratorical abilities of Winston Churchill and the intellectual capacities of Albert Einstein, you can still improve your teaching skills . . . and you should.

God's gifts are no guarantee of success; they must be cultivated and nurtured; otherwise they diminish over time. Today, accept this challenge: value the gift that God has given you, nourish it, make it grow, and share it with your students and with the world. After all, the best way to say "Thank You" for God's gifts is to use them.

———————

God is still in the process of dispensing gifts, and He uses ordinary individuals like us to develop those gifts in other people.

Howard Hendricks

———————

Heavenly Father, Your gifts to me are priceless and eternal. I praise You and give thanks for Your creation, for Your Son, and for the unique talents and opportunities that You have given me. Let me use my gifts for the glory of Your kingdom, this day and every day. Amen

GOD'S BLESSINGS

The Lord bless you and protect you; the Lord make His face shine on you, and be gracious to you.

Numbers 6:24-25 HCSB

Blessings are on the head of the righteous.

Proverbs 10:6 HCSB

Come to terms with God and be at peace; in this way good will come to you.

Job 22:21 HCSB

Blessed is a man who endures trials, because when he passes the test he will receive the crown of life that He has promised to those who love Him.

James 1:12 HCSB

I will give you a new heart and put a new spirit within you.

Ezekiel 36:26 HCSB

Have you counted your blessings lately? If you sincerely wish to follow in Christ's footsteps, you should make thanksgiving a habit, a regular part of your daily routine.

How has God blessed you? First and foremost, He has given you the gift of eternal life through the sacrifice of His only begotten Son, but the blessings don't stop there. Today, take time to make a partial list of God's gifts to you: the talents, the opportunities, the possessions, and the relationships that you may, on occasion, take for granted. And then, when you've spent sufficient time listing your blessings, offer a prayer of gratitude to the Giver of all things good . . . and, to the best of your ability, use your gifts for the glory of His kingdom.

Today, Lord, let me count my blessings with thanksgiving in my heart. You have cared for me, Lord, and I will give You the glory and the praise. Let me accept Your blessings and Your gifts, and let me share them with my students, just as You first shared them with me. Amen

GOD'S
COMMANDMENTS

Happy are those who fear the Lord. Yes, happy are those who delight in doing what he commands.

Psalm 112:1 NLT

For this is the love of God, that we keep his commandments . . . .

1 John 5:3 KJV

Whoso despiseth the word shall be destroyed: but he that feareth the commandment shall be rewarded.

Proverbs 13:13 KJV

He that hath my commandments, and keepeth them, he it is that loveth me: and he that loveth me shall be loved of my Father, and I will love him, and will manifest myself to him.

John 14:21 KJV

Jesus answered and said unto him, If a man love me, he will keep my words: and my Father will love him, and we will come unto him, and make our abode with him.

John 14:23 KJV

A righteous life has many components: faith, honesty, generosity, discipline, love, kindness, humility, gratitude, and worship, to name but a few. If we seek to follow the steps of Jesus, we must seek to live according to His commandments. In short, we must, to the best of our abilities, live according to the principles contained in God's Holy Word. And then, through our words and our deeds, we must teach our students to do the same.

———

Let us remember therefore this lesson: That to worship our God sincerely we must evermore begin by hearkening to His voice, and by giving ear to what He commands us. For if every man goes after his own way, we shall wander. We may well run, but we shall never be a whit nearer to the right way, but rather farther away from it.

John Calvin

———

Lord, Your commandments are a perfect guide for my life; let me obey them, and let me teach others to do the same. Give me the wisdom to walk righteously in Your way, Dear Lord, trusting always in You. Amen

GOD'S GRACE

You therefore, my son, be strong in the grace that is in Christ Jesus.

2 Timothy 2:1 NKJV

And God raised us up with Christ and seated us with him in the heavenly realms in Christ Jesus, in order that in the coming ages he might show the incomparable riches of his grace, expressed in his kindness to us in Christ Jesus.

Ephesians 2:6-7 NIV

For the law was given through Moses; grace and truth came through Jesus Christ.

John 1:17 NIV

My grace is sufficient for you, for my power is made perfect in weakness.

2 Corinthians 12:9 NIV

But by the grace of God I am what I am, and his grace to me was not without effect.

1 Corinthians 15:10 NIV

W e have received countless gifts from God, but none can compare with the gift of salvation. When we accept Christ into our hearts, we are saved by God's grace. The familiar words of Ephesians 2:8 make God's promise perfectly clear: we are saved, not by our actions, but by God's mercy. We are saved, not because of our good deeds, but because of our faith in Christ.

God's grace is the ultimate gift, and we owe Him the ultimate in thanksgiving. Let us praise the Creator for His priceless gift, and let us share the Good News with all who cross our paths. We return our Father's love by accepting His grace and by sharing His message and His love. When we do, we are blessed here on earth and throughout all eternity.

Dear Lord, You have offered Your grace freely through Christ Jesus. I praise You for that priceless gift. Let me share the good news of Your Son with a world that desperately needs His peace, His abundance, His love, and His salvation. Amen

GOD'S LOVE

For the LORD your God has arrived to live among you. He is a mighty savior. He will rejoice over you with great gladness. With his love, he will calm all your fears. He will exult over you by singing a happy song.

Zephaniah 3:17 NLT

But God demonstrates His own love toward us, in that while we were still sinners, Christ died for us.

Romans 5:8 NKJV

For he chose us in him before the creation of the world to be holy and blameless in his sight. In love he predestined us to be adopted as his sons through Jesus Christ, in accordance with his pleasure and will . . . .

Ephesians 1:4-5 NIV

For God so loved the world that he gave his only Son, so that everyone who believes in him will not perish but have eternal life.

John 3:16 NLT

Unfailing love surrounds those who trust the LORD.

Psalm 32:10 NLT

God's love changes lives. And as Christian teachers who have received the priceless gift of God's grace, we must make certain that our students can clearly see the changes that God has made in us. Can we be perfect teachers? Of course not. Can we, at all times, be patient, kind, calm, and loving? That's highly unlikely. What we can do is this: we can demonstrate to our students that Christ's love does indeed make a difference in the lives of those who accept Him as their Savior.

God's grace is the ultimate gift, and we owe Him the ultimate in thanksgiving. Let us praise the Creator for His priceless gift; let us share His Good News; and let us live according to His commandments. When we do, our students will be blessed with powerful, godly role models. And we teachers will be transformed, not only for a day, but also for all eternity.

———

Dear Lord, for the love You have shown me and the blessings You have given me, I thank You and I praise You. Your Son died so that I might receive the blessing of eternal love and eternal life. I will praise You today, tomorrow, and forever, Lord, for Your love, for Your mercy, and for Your Son. Amen

GOD'S PLAN

And we know that in all things God works for the good of those who love him, who have been called according to his purpose.

Romans 8:28 NIV

The steps of the Godly are directed by the Lord. He delights in every detail of their lives. Though they stumble, they will not fall, for the Lord holds them by the hand.

Psalm 37:23-24 NLT

It is God who works in you to will and to act according to his good purpose.

Philippians 2:13 NIV

"For I know the plans I have for you," declares the Lord, "plans to prosper you and not to harm you, plans to give you hope and a future. Then you will call upon me and come and pray to me, and I will listen to you."

Jeremiah 29:11-12 NIV

Who are those who fear the Lord? He will show them the path they should choose. They will live in prosperity, and their children will inherit the Promised Land.

Psalm 25:12-13 NLT

God has important plans for your life and for the lives of your students. But He won't force His plans upon you. To the contrary, He has given all of His children free will (a fact that is not lost on any teacher who has ever tried to quiet an unruly classroom).

While you, as a concerned teacher, can encourage your students to seek purpose and meaning for their own lives, you can't force them to do so. You can, however, seek to discover God's plan for your life. God is listening and waiting for you to reach out to Him, and He intends to use you in wonderful, unexpected ways. So let Him.

Nothing happens by happenstance. I am not in the hands of fate, nor am I the victim of man's whims or the devil's ploys. There is One who sits above man, above Satan, and above all heavenly hosts as the ultimate authority of all the universe. That One is my God and my Father!

Kay Arthur

Dear Lord, You have a plan for my life. Let me discover it and live it. And, let me help others seek Your will. Today, I will seek the wisdom of Your perfect plan, Father, knowing that when I trust in You, I am eternally blessed. Amen

GOD'S TIMING

He has made everything beautiful in its time. He has also set eternity in the hearts of men; yet they cannot fathom what God has done from beginning to end.

Ecclesiastes 3:11 NIV

Yet the LORD longs to be gracious to you; he rises to show you compassion. For the LORD is a God of justice. Blessed are all who wait for him!

Isaiah 30:18 NIV

I wait for the LORD, my soul waits, and in his word I put my hope.

Psalm 130:5 NIV

I waited patiently for the LORD; And He inclined to me, And heard my cry.

Psalm 40:1 NKJV

He [Jesus] said to them: "It is not for you to know the times or dates the Father has set by his own authority."

Acts 1:7 NIV

S tudents, as a whole, can be quite impatient. They can't wait for class to end; ditto for the school day and the school week. They wait impatiently for Christmas vacation, spring break, and—most urgently—summer vacation. But, wise teachers understand that life beyond the classroom requires patience, patience, and more patience.

Unlike the precisely charted school year, life unfolds according to a timetable that is ordained, not by man, but by God. Let us, as believers, wait patiently for God, and let us teach patience to those who look to us for guidance . . . even if they're squirming in their seats, waiting for the bell to ring.

———

Your times are in His hands. He's in charge of the timetable, so wait patiently.

Kay Arthur

———

Dear Lord, Your wisdom is infinite, and the timing of Your heavenly plan is perfect. You have a plan for my life that is grander than I can imagine. When I am impatient, remind me that You are never early or late. You are always on time, Father, so let me trust in You. Amen

GOSSIP

The whole point of what we're urging is simply love—love uncontaminated by self-interest and counterfeit faith, a life open to God. Those who fail to keep to this point soon wander off into cul-de-sacs of gossip.

1 Timothy 1:5-6 MSG

Though some tongues just love the taste of gossip, Christians have better uses for language than that. Don't talk dirty or silly. That kind of talk doesn't fit our style. Thanksgiving is our dialect.

Ephesians 5:4 MSG

If anyone considers himself religious and yet does not keep a tight rein on his tongue, he deceives himself and his religion is worthless.

James 1:26 NIV

When we put bits into the mouths of horses to make them obey us, we can control their whole bodies. Also a ship is very big, and it is pushed by strong winds. But a very small rudder controls that big ship, making it go wherever the pilot wants. It is the same with the tongue. It is a small part of the body, but it brags about great things. A big forest fire can be started with only a little flame.

James 3:3-5 NCV

D o you know what gossip is? It's when we say bad things about people who are not around to hear us. When we say bad things about other people, we hurt them and we hurt ourselves. That's why the Bible tells us that gossip is wrong.

When we say things that we don't want other people to know we said, we're being somewhat dishonest, but if the things we say aren't true, we're being very dishonest. Either way, we have done something that we may regret later, especially if the other person finds out.

So do yourself a big favor: don't gossip. It's a waste of words, and it's the wrong thing to do. You'll feel better about yourself if you don't gossip about other people. So don't do it!

Never utter in your neighbor's absence what you wouldn't say in his presence.

Mary Magdalene di Pazzi

Dear Lord, it's tempting to gossip, but it's wrong. Today and every day, help me speak words that are pleasing to You, and help me treat other people in the same way that I want to be treated by them. Amen

GRATITUDE

As you therefore have received Christ Jesus the Lord, so walk in Him, having been firmly rooted and now being built up in Him and established in your faith, just as you were instructed, and overflowing with gratitude.

Colossians 2:6-7 NASB

Therefore, since we receive a kingdom which cannot be shaken, let us show gratitude, by which we may offer to God an acceptable service with reverence and awe . . . .

Hebrews 12:28 NASB

It is good to give thanks to the Lord, to sing praises to the Most High. It is good to proclaim your unfailing love in the morning, your faithfulness in the evening.

Psalm 92:1-2 NLT

Everything created by God is good, and nothing is to be rejected, if it is received with gratitude; for it is sanctified by means of the word of God and prayer.

1 Timothy 4:4-5 NASB

As teachers, we have responsibilities that begin long before the school bell rings and end long after the last student has left the classroom. Amid the hustle and bustle of the daily grind, it is easy to lose sight of God and His blessings. But, when we forget to slow down and say "Thank You" to our Creator, we rob ourselves of His presence, His peace, and His joy.

Our task, as believing Christians, is to praise God many times each day. Then, with gratitude in our hearts, we can face our daily duties with the perspective and power that only He can provide.

———

A sense of gratitude for God's presence in our lives will help open our eyes to what he has done in the past and what he will do in the future.

Emilie Barnes

———

Lord, let my attitude be one of gratitude. You have given me much; when I think of Your grace and goodness, I am humbled and thankful. Today, let me express my thanksgiving, Father, not just through my words but also through my deeds . . . and may all the glory be Yours. Amen

God's Promises About . . .

HAPPINESS

But the truly happy person is the one who carefully studies God's perfect law that makes people free. He continues to study it. He listens to God's teaching and does not forget what he heard. Then he obeys what God's teaching says. When he does this, it makes him happy.

James 1:25 ICB

Happy are those who fear the Lord. Yes, happy are those who delight in doing what he commands.

Psalm 112:1 NLT

Delight thyself also in the LORD; and he shall give thee the desires of thine heart.

Psalm 37:4 KJV

How happy are those who can live in your house, always singing your praises. How happy are those who are strong in the Lord . . . .

Psalm 84:4-5 NLT

Always be happy. Never stop praying. Give thanks whatever happens. That is what God wants for you in Christ Jesus.

1 Thessalonians 5:16-18 ICB

D o you seek happiness, abundance, and contentment? If so, here are some things you should do: Love God and His Son; depend upon God for strength; try, to the best of your abilities, to follow God's will; and strive to obey His Holy Word. When you do these things, you'll discover that happiness goes hand-in-hand with righteousness. The happiest people are not those who rebel against God; the happiest people are those who love God and obey His commandments.

What does life have in store for you? A world full of possibilities (of course it's up to you to seize them), and God's promise of abundance (of course it's up to you to accept it). So, as you embark upon the next phase of your journey, remember to celebrate the life that God has given you. Your Creator has blessed you beyond measure. Honor Him with your prayers, your words, your deeds, and your joy.

Lord, let me be a teacher who celebrates life. Let me rejoice in the gift of this day, and let me praise You for the gift of Your Son. Let me be a joyful Christian, Lord, as I share Your Good News with friends, with family, and with the world. Amen

HELPING OTHERS

You address me as "Teacher" and "Master," and rightly so. That is what I am. So if I, the Master and Teacher, washed your feet, you must now wash each other's feet. I've laid down a pattern for you. What I've done, you do.

John 13:15 MSG

The one who blesses others is abundantly blessed; those who help others are helped.

Proverbs 11:25 MSG

Whenever you are able, do good to people who need help.

Proverbs 3:27 NCV

When we have the opportunity to help anyone, we should do it. But we should give special attention to those who are in the family of believers.

Galatians 6:10 NCV

J esus told the story of the "Good Samaritan," a man who helped a fellow traveler when no one else would. We, too, should be good Samaritans when we find people who need our help.

Zora Neale Hurston noted, "When you find a man who has lost his way, you don't make fun of him and scorn him and leave him there. You show him the way. If you don't do that you just prove that you're sort of lost yourself."

And Helen Keller advised, "Believe, when you are most unhappy, that there is something for you to do in the world. So long as you can sweeten another's pain, life is not in vain."

So today, find somebody who needs a hug or a helping hand . . . and give them both.

Unless our belief in God causes us to help our fellowmen, our faith stands condemned.

Billy Graham

Dear Lord, let me help others in every way that I can. Jesus served others; I can too. I will serve other people with my good deeds and with my prayers, today and every day. Amen

HONESTY

Therefore laying aside falsehood, speak truth, each one of you, with his neighbor, for we are members of one another.

Ephesians 4:25 NASB

But when he, the Spirit of truth, comes, he will guide you into all truth . . . .

John 16:13 NIV

Jesus answered, "I am the way and the truth and the life. No one comes to the Father except through me."

John 14:6 NIV

And ye shall know the truth, and the truth shall make you free.

John 8:32 KJV

As we have received mercy, we faint not; but have renounced the hidden things of dishonesty, not walking in craftiness, nor handling the word of God deceitfully; but, by manifestation of the truth, commending ourselves to every man's conscience in the sight of God.

2 Corinthians 4:1-2 KJV

Wise teachers understand the importance of character . . . and teach it. Character is built slowly over a lifetime. It is the sum of every right decision, every honest word, every noble thought, and every heartfelt prayer. It is forged on the anvil of honorable work and polished by the twin virtues of generosity and humility. Character is a precious thing—difficult to build but easy to tear down; godly teachers value it and protect it at all costs . . . and they encourage their students to do the same.

———————

God doesn't expect you to be perfect, but he does insist on complete honesty.

Rick Warren

———————

Dear Lord, let me walk in truth and let me share Your truth. As a teacher, I am a role model to my students. Make me Your worthy servant so that others might see my love for You reflected in my words and my deeds. Amen

HOPE

Be joyful in hope, patient in affliction, faithful in prayer.

Romans 12:12 NIV

The Lord is good to those whose hope is in him, to the one who seeks him; it is good to wait quietly for the salvation of the Lord.

Lamentations 3:25-26 NIV

Blessed is he whose help is the God of Jacob, whose hope is in the LORD his God, the Maker of heaven and earth, the sea, and everything in them—the LORD, who remains faithful forever.

Psalm 146:5-6 NIV

May the God of hope fill you with all joy and peace as you trust in him, so that you may overflow with hope by the power of the Holy Spirit.

Romans 15:13 NIV

Be of good courage, and he shall strengthen your heart, all ye that hope in the LORD.

Psalm 31:24 KJV

Along with other lessons, we must teach our students the wisdom of hope. There are few sadder sights than that of a thoroughly discouraged young person. As teachers, we cannot control the emotions of our students, but we can help our students learn to think optimistically about themselves and about their opportunities.

Hope, like plants in a garden, must be cultivated with care. If we leave our hopes untended—or if we contaminate them with the twin poisons of discouragement and doubt—the gardens of our soul produce few fruits. But, if we nurture our hopes through a firm faith in God and a realistic faith in ourselves, we bring forth bountiful harvests that bless us, our families, ours students, and generations yet unborn.

———

Dear Lord, make me a teacher of hope. If I become discouraged, let me turn to You. If I grow weary, let me seek strength in You. When I face adversity, let me seek Your will and trust Your Word. In every aspect of my life, I will trust You, Father, so that my heart will be filled with faith and hope, this day and forever. Amen

God's Promises About . . .

JESUS

For Jesus is the one referred to in the Scriptures, where it says, "The stone that you builders rejected has now become the cornerstone." There is salvation in no one else! There is no other name in all of heaven for people to call on to save them.

Acts 4:11-12 NLT

Let us run with endurance the race that is set before us, fixing our eyes on Jesus, the author and perfecter of faith, who for the joy set before Him endured the cross, despising the shame, and has sat down at the right hand of the throne of God.

Hebrews 12:1-2 NASB

Jesus Christ the same yesterday, and today, and for ever.

Hebrews 13:8 KJV

I am the Vine, you are the branches. When you're joined with me and I with you, the relation intimate and organic, the harvest is sure to be abundant.

John 15:5 MSG

Who was the greatest teacher in the history of the world? Jesus was . . . and He still is! Jesus teaches us how to live, how to behave, and how to worship. Now, it's up to each of us, as Christians, to learn the important lessons that Jesus can teach.

Some day soon, you will have learned everything that Jesus has to teach you, right? WRONG!!!! Jesus will keep teaching you important lessons throughout your life. And that's good, because all of us, kids and grown-ups alike, have lots to learn . . . especially from the Master . . . and the Master, of course, is Jesus.

———

Jesus Christ is the One by whom, for whom, through whom everything was made. Therefore, He knows what's wrong in your life, and He knows how to fix it.

Anne Graham Lotz

———

Dear Heavenly Father, I praise You and thank You for Your priceless gift: Jesus Christ. Let me share the Good News of the One who became a man so that I might become His, not only for today, but also for all eternity. Jesus is my Savior and my strength. I will welcome Him into my heart with love and thanksgiving, today and forever. Amen

JOY

*Thou wilt show me the path of life: in thy presence is fulness of joy;
at thy right hand there are pleasures for evermore.*

Psalm 16:11 KJV

Weeping may endure for a night, but joy cometh in the morning.

Psalm 30:5 KJV

*I will thank you, Lord, with all my heart; I will tell of all the
marvelous things you have done. I will be filled with joy because of
you. I will sing praises to your name, O Most High.*

Psalm 9:1-2 NLT

*Delight thyself also in the LORD; and he shall give thee the desires
of thine heart.*

Psalm 37:4 KJV

*Rejoice, and be exceeding glad: for great is your reward in
heaven . . . .*

Matthew 5:12 KJV

Teaching should be a joyful experience, but every teacher knows that some days are so busy and so hurried that abundance seems a distant promise. It is not. Every day, we can claim the spiritual abundance and joy that God promises for our lives . . . and we should.

C. H. Spurgeon, the renowned 19th-century English clergymen, advised, "Rejoicing is clearly a spiritual command. To ignore it, I need to remind you, is disobedience." As Christians, we are called by our Creator to live abundantly, prayerfully, and joyfully. To do otherwise is to squander His spiritual gifts.

If, today, your heart is heavy, open the door of your soul to the Father and to His only begotten Son. Christ offers you His peace and His joy. Accept it and share it freely, just as Christ has freely shared His joy with you.

Lord, make me a joyous Christian. Because of my salvation through Your Son, I have every reason to celebrate—let my joy be evident in every aspect of life, including my life inside the classroom. Today, let my words and deeds be a testimony to Christ's love and to His grace. Amen

KINDNESS

May the Lord cause you to increase and abound in love for one another, and for all people.

1 Thessalonians 3:12 NASB

And be ye kind one to another, tenderhearted, forgiving one another, even as God for Christ's sake hath forgiven you.

Ephesians 4:32 KJV

Verily I say unto you, Inasmuch as ye have done it unto one of the least of these my brethren, ye have done it unto me.

Matthew 25:40 KJV

Be ye therefore merciful, as your Father also is merciful.

Luke 6:36 KJV

Show respect for all people. Love the brothers and sisters of God's family.

1 Peter 2:17 ICB

In the busyness and stress of a teacher's demanding day, it is easy to become frustrated. We are imperfect human beings struggling to manage our lives as best we can, but sometimes we fall short. When we are distracted or disappointed, we may neglect to share a kind word or a kind deed. This oversight hurts others, and it hurts us as well.

Christ's words are straightforward: "I tell you the truth, anything you did for even the least of my people here, you also did for me" (Matthew 25:40 NCV). For believers, then, the message is clear: When we share a word of encouragement with a student or extend the hand of friendship to a peer, God smiles.

Kindness in this world will do much to help others, not only to come into the light, but also to grow in grace day by day.

Fanny Crosby

Lord, make me a loving, encouraging Christian. And, let my love for Christ be reflected through the kindness that I show to my students, to my family, to my friends, and to all who need the healing touch of the Master's hand. Amen

KNOWLEDGE

It is not good to have zeal without knowledge, nor to be hasty and miss the way.

Proverbs 19:2 NIV

The fear of the Lord is the beginning of knowledge, but fools despise wisdom and discipline.

Proverbs 1:7 NIV

The lips of the wise spread knowledge; not so the hearts of fools.

Proverbs 15:7 NIV

The knowledge of the secrets of the kingdom of heaven has been given to you....

Matthew 13:11 NIV

By wisdom a house is built, and through understanding it is established; through knowledge its rooms are filled with rare and beautiful treasures.

Proverbs 24:3-4 NIV

Our children need both knowledge and wisdom. Knowledge is found in textbooks. Wisdom, on the other hand, is found in God's Holy Word and in the carefully chosen words of loving parents and thoughtful teachers. When we give our children the gift of knowledge, we do them a wonderful service. But, when we share the gift of wisdom, we offer a timeless treasure that surpasses knowledge and reshapes eternity.

———

A little knowledge turns one away from God; a great deal of knowledge brings one back to him.

St. Monica

———

Lord, You are my Teacher. Help me to be a student of Your Word and a servant of Your will. Let me live by the truth You reveal, let me trust in the wisdom of Your commandments, and let me teach others the glory of Your ways. Amen

LEADERSHIP

Shepherd God's flock among you, not overseeing out of compulsion but freely, according to God's will; not for the money but eagerly.

1 Peter 5:2 HCSB

An overseer, therefore, must be above reproach, the husband of one wife, self-controlled, sensible, respectable, hospitable, an able teacher, not addicted to wine, not a bully but gentle, not quarrelsome, not greedy.

1 Timothy 3:2-3 HCSB

His master said to him, "Well done, good and faithful slave! You were faithful over a few things; I will put you in charge of many things. Enter your master's joy!"

Matthew 25:21 HCSB

According to the grace given to us, we have different gifts: If prophecy, use it according to the standard of faith; if service, in service; if teaching, in teaching; if exhorting, in exhortation; giving, with generosity; leading, with diligence; showing mercy, with cheerfulness.

Romans 12:6-8 HCSB

As a teacher, you are automatically placed in a position of leadership. Unless, you assume firm control over your students, effective learning will not take place in your classroom.

John Maxwell writes, "Great leaders understand that the right attitude will set the right atmosphere, which enables the right response from others." As the leader of your class, it's up to you to set the proper balance between discipline and amusement, between entertainment and scholarship.

Savvy teachers learn to strike an appropriate balance between discipline (which is necessary for maintaining order) and fun (which is necessary for maintaining interest). The rest, of course, is up to the students.

You can never separate a leader's actions from his character.

John Maxwell

Dear Lord, let me be a leader in my classroom and a worthy example to my students. Give me wisdom, courage, compassion, and faith. Let me turn to You, Father, for guidance and for strength in all that I say and do. Amen

LIFE

His divine power has given us everything we need for life and godliness through our knowledge of him who called us by his own glory and goodness.

2 Peter 1:3 NIV

Seek the Lord, and ye shall live . . . .

Amos 5:6 KJV

I urge you to live a life worthy of the calling you have received.

Ephesians 4:1 NIV

And Jesus said unto them, I am the bread of life: he that cometh to me shall never hunger; and he that believeth on me shall never thirst.

John 6:35 KJV

Watch your life and doctrine closely. Persevere in them, because if you do, you will save both yourself and your hearers.

1 Timothy 4:16 NIV

L ife is God's gift to you, and He intends that you celebrate His glorious gift. If you're a teacher who treasures each day—and if you encourage your students to do the same—you will be blessed by your Father in heaven.

Christian believers face the inevitable challenges and disappointments of each day armed with the joy of Christ and the promise of salvation. So whatever this day holds for you, begin it and end it with God as your partner and Christ as your Savior. And throughout the day, give thanks to the One who created you and saved you. God's love for you is infinite. Accept it joyously and be thankful.

———

Live in such a way that any day would make a suitable capstone for life. Live so that you need not change your mode of living, even if your sudden departure were immediately predicted to you.

C. H. Spurgeon

———

Lord, You have given me the gift of life. Let me treasure it, and let me use it for Your service and for Your glory. Amen

LOVING GOD

This is love: not that we loved God, but that he loved us and sent his Son as an atoning sacrifice for our sins.

1 John 4:10 NIV

Love the LORD your God with all your heart and with all your soul and with all your strength.

Deuteronomy 6:5 NIV

I will sing of the LORD's great love forever; with my mouth I will make your faithfulness known through all generations.

Psalm 89:1 NIV

And we know that in all things God works for the good of those who love him, who have been called according to his purpose.

Romans 8:28 NIV

We love him, because he first loved us.

1 John 4:19 KJV

If you want to know God in a more meaningful way, you'll need to open up your heart and let Him in. C. S. Lewis observed, "A person's spiritual health is exactly proportional to his love for God." If you hope to receive a full measure of God's spiritual blessings, you must invite your Creator to rule over your heart. When you honor God in this way, His love expands to fill your heart and bless your life.

St. Augustine wrote, "I love you, Lord, not doubtingly, but with absolute certainty. Your Word beat upon my heart until I fell in love with you, and now the universe and everything in it tells me to love you."

Today, open your heart to the Father. And let your obedience be a fitting response to His never-ending love.

―――――――

When our heart's desire is to please our Lord because we love Him, there will be no time for second thoughts or second opinions.

Warren Wiersbe

―――――――

Dear Heavenly Father, You have blessed me with a love that is infinite and eternal. Let me love You, Lord, more and more each day. Make me a loving servant, Father, today and throughout eternity. And, let me show my love for You by sharing Your message and Your love with others. Amen

LOVING OTHERS

Jesus replied, "'Love the Lord your God with all your heart and with all your soul and with all your mind.' This is the first and greatest commandment. And the second is like it: 'Love your neighbor as yourself.' All the Law and the Prophets hang on these two commandments."

Matthew 22:37-40 NIV

And the Lord make you to increase and abound in love one toward another, and toward all men . . . .

1 Thessalonians 3:12 KJV

Above all, love each other deeply, because love covers over a multitude of sins.

1 Peter 4:8 NIV

Love one another deeply, from the heart.

1 Peter 1:22 NIV

And he has given us this command: Whoever loves God must also love his brother.

1 John 4:21 NIV

The beautiful words of 1st Corinthians 13 remind us that love is God's commandment: "But now abide faith, hope, love, these three; but the greatest of these is love" (v. 13 NASB). Faith is important, of course. So, too, is hope. But, love is more important still. Christ showed His love for us on the cross, and, as Christians, we are called upon to return Christ's love by sharing it. Today, let us spread Christ's love to families, friends, and strangers by word and by deed.

———

God loves me as God loves all people, without qualification. . . . To be in the image of God means that all of us are made for the purpose of knowing and loving God and one another and of being loved in turn, not literally in the same way God knows and loves, but in a way appropriate to human beings.

Roberta Bondi

———

Dear Lord, Your love for me is infinite and eternal. Let me acknowledge Your love, accept Your love, and share Your love. Make me a teacher who demonstrates compassion, understanding, and forgiveness. And let the love that I feel in my heart be expressed through kind words, good deeds, and heartfelt prayers. Amen

MATURITY

Consider it pure joy, my brothers, whenever you face trials of many kinds, because you know that the testing of your faith develops perseverance. Perseverance must finish its work so that you may be mature and complete, not lacking anything.

James 1:2-4 NIV

But grow in the grace and knowledge of our Lord and Savior Jesus Christ.

2 Peter 3:18 NIV

Therefore let us leave the elementary teachings about Christ and go on to maturity . . . .

Hebrews 6:1 NIV

There has never been the slightest doubt in my mind that the God who started this great work in you would keep at it and bring it to a flourishing finish on the very day Christ Jesus appears.

Philippians 1:6 MSG

When I was a child, I spoke and thought and reasoned as a child does. But when I grew up, I put away childish things.

1 Corinthians 13:11 NLT

If only our students would behave maturely and responsibly, teaching would be a breeze. But, here in the real world, young people don't grow into mature adults overnight. What's a teacher to do? Be patient, be understanding, and be demanding. Teachers who allow undisciplined behavior to go unchecked are doing a disservice to their students. God does not reward laziness nor does He praise mediocrity, and neither should we.

God cannot build character without our cooperation. If we resist Him, then He chastens us into submission. But, if we submit to Him, then He can accomplish His work. He is not satisfied with a halfway job. God wants a perfect work; He wants a finished product that is mature and complete.

Warren Wiersbe

Dear Lord, let me grow in Your wisdom. When I study Your Word and follow Your commandments, I become a more mature Christian and a more effective teacher. Let me grow up, Lord, and let me keep growing up every day that I live. Amen

MENTORS

My dear brothers and sisters, if anyone among you wanders away from the truth and is brought back again, you can be sure that the one who brings that person back will save that sinner from death and bring about the forgiveness of many sins.

James 5:19-20 NLT

If you help, just help, don't take over; if you teach, stick to your teaching; if you give encouraging guidance, be careful that you don't get bossy; if you're put in charge, don't manipulate; if you're called to give aid to people in distress, keep your eyes open and be quick to respond; if you work with the disadvantaged, don't let yourself get irritated with them or depressed by them. Keep a smile on your face. Love from the center of who you are; don't fake it. Run for dear life from evil; hold on for dear life to good.

Romans 12:7-9 MSG

Listen to advice and accept correction, and in the end you will be wise.

Proverbs 19:20 NCV

The one who walks with the wise will become wise, but a companion of fools will suffer harm.

Proverbs 13:20 HCSB

Do you wish to become a better teacher and a wiser person? Then you must walk with people who, by their words and their presence, make you wiser. But that's not all; you must avoid those people who encourage you to think foolish thoughts or do foolish things.

Today, as a gift to yourself, select, from your friends and coworkers, a mentor whose judgement you trust. Then listen carefully to your mentor's advice and be willing to accept that advice, even if accepting it requires effort or pain, or both. Consider your mentor to be God's gift to you. Thank God for that gift, and treasure the wisdom that you gain.

And what should you do with all that hard-earned knowledge that you acquire from your mentor? Share it, of course, with the students and coworkers who are wise enough to learn from you.

———

Lord, make me a wise counselor to those whom I teach. Make me a worthy mentor and a godly example to my students. Let me lead them in the ways of wisdom, discipline, and righteousness by the words that I speak and the way that I live my life. Amen

God's Promises About . . .

MIRACLES

Now glory be to God! By his mighty power at work within us, he is able to accomplish infinitely more than we would ever dare to ask or hope.

Ephesians 3:20 NLT

God verified the message by signs and wonders and various miracles and by giving gifts of the Holy Spirit whenever he chose to do so.

Hebrews 2:4 NLT

Jesus said to them, "I have shown you many great miracles from the Father."

John 10:32 NIV

The person who trusts me will not only do what I'm doing but even greater things, because I, on my way to the Father, am giving you the same work to do that I've been doing.

John 14:12 MSG

But as it is written: "Eye has not seen, nor ear heard, nor have entered into the heart of man the things which God has prepared for those who love Him."

1 Corinthians 2:9 NKJV

When, at the age of two, she was stricken with what 19th-century doctors called "brain fever," Helen Keller was left deaf and blind. Keller might have been excused for having a sour attitude about life, but she did not give in to the paralysis of bitterness and despair. Instead, with the help of an extraordinary teacher named Anne Sullivan, young Helen learned to communicate and quickly embraced education.

Eventually, Keller graduated with a cum laude degree from Radcliffe, and then went on to become a noted American writer and lecturer. She once observed, "When we do the best we can, we never know what miracles await."

What miracles await you? Big ones! When you do your part, God will do His part, and the results will be . . . miraculous!

Dear God, nothing is impossible for You. Your infinite power is beyond human understanding—keep me always mindful of Your strength. When I lose hope, give me faith; when others lose hope, let me teach of Your glory and Your works. Today, Lord, let me expect the miraculous, and let me trust in You. Amen

MISTAKES

You were taught, with regard to your former way of life, to put off your old self, which is being corrupted by its deceitful desires; to be made new in the attitude of your minds; and to put on the new self, created to be like God in true righteousness and holiness.

Ephesians 4:22-24 NIV

If we confess our sins, he is faithful and just and will forgive us our sins and purify us from all unrighteousness.

1 John 1:9 NIV

Have mercy on me, O God, according to your unfailing love; according to your great compassion blot out my transgressions. Wash away all my iniquity and cleanse me from my sin.

Psalm 51:1-2 NIV

I waited patiently for the LORD; he turned to me and heard my cry. He lifted me out of the slimy pit, out of the mud and mire; he set my feet on a rock and gave me a firm place to stand. He put a new song in my mouth, a hymn of praise to our God . . . .

Psalm 40:1-3 NIV

We are imperfect beings living in an imperfect world; mistakes are simply part of the price we pay for being here. Yet, even though mistakes are an inevitable part of life's journey, repeated mistakes should not be. When we commit the inevitable blunders of life, we must correct them, learn from them, and pray for the wisdom to avoid those same mistakes in the future. If we are successful, our missteps become lessons, and our lives become adventures in growth.

Mistakes are the price we pay for being human; repeated mistakes are the price we pay for being stubborn. But, if we are wise enough to learn from our experiences, we continue to mature throughout every stage of life. And that's precisely what God intends for us to do.

———

Lord, I know that I am imperfect and that I fail You in many ways. Thank You for Your forgiveness and for Your unconditional love. Show me the error of my ways, Lord, that I might confess my wrongdoing and correct my mistakes. And, let me grow each day in wisdom, in faith, and in my love for You. Amen

God's Promises About . . .

OPPORTUNITIES

Make the most of every opportunity.

Colossians 4:5 NIV

Let us not lose heart in doing good, for in due time we shall reap if we do not grow weary. So then, while we have opportunity, let us do good to all men, and especially to those who are of the household of the faith.

Galatians 6:9-10 NASB

Dear brothers and sisters, whenever trouble comes your way, let it be an opportunity for joy. For when your faith is tested, your endurance has a chance to grow. So let it grow, for when your endurance is fully developed, you will be strong in character and ready for anything.

James 1:2-4 NLT

I can do everything through him who gives me strength.

Philippians 4:13 NIV

Are you excited about the opportunities of today and thrilled by the possibilities of tomorrow? Do you confidently expect God to lead you to a place of abundance, peace, and joy? And, when your days on earth are over, do you expect to receive the priceless gift of eternal life? If you trust God's promises, and if you have welcomed God's Son into your heart, then you believe that your future is intensely and eternally bright.

Today, as you prepare to meet the duties of everyday life, pause and consider God's promises. And then think for a moment about the wonderful future that awaits all believers, including you. God has promised that your future is secure. Trust that promise, and celebrate the life of abundance and eternal joy that is now yours through Christ.

With the right attitude and a willingness to pay the price, almost anyone can pursue nearly any opportunity and achieve it.

John Maxwell

Lord, as I take the next steps on my life's journey, let me take them with You. Whatever this day may bring, I thank You for the opportunity to live abundantly. Let me lean upon You, Father—and trust You—this day and forever. Amen

OPTIMISM

I can do everything through him that gives me strength.

Philippians 4:13 NIV

Be of good courage, and he shall strengthen your heart, all ye that hope in the LORD.

Psalm 31:24 KJV

Summing it all up, friends, I'd say you'll do best by filling your minds and meditating on things true, noble, reputable, authentic, compelling, gracious, the best, not the worst; the beautiful, not the ugly; things to praise, not things to curse. Put into practice what you learned from me, what you heard and saw and realized. Do that, and God, who makes everything work together, will work you into his most excellent harmonies.

Philippians 4:8-9 MSG

The Lord is my light and my salvation; whom shall I fear? The Lord is the strength of my life; of whom shall I be afraid?

Psalm 27:1 KJV

Christians have every reason to be optimistic about life. As John Calvin observed, "There is not one blade of grass, there is no color in this world that is not intended to make us rejoice." But sometimes, when we are tired or frustrated, rejoicing seems only a distant promise. Thankfully, God stands ready to restore us: "I will give you a new heart and put a new spirit in you . . ." (Ezekiel 36:26 NIV). Our task, of course, is to let Him.

Today, accept the new spirit that God seeks to infuse into your heart. Think optimistically about yourself, your students, your school, and your world. Rejoice in this glorious day that the Lord has given you, and share your optimism with others. Your enthusiasm will be contagious, and your words will bring healing and comfort to a world that needs both.

Change your thoughts, and you change your world.

Norman Vincent Peale

Lord, give me faith, optimism, and hope. Let me expect the best from You, and let me look for the best in my students. Let me trust You, Lord, to direct my life. And, let me be Your faithful, hopeful, optimistic servant every day that I live. Amen

PASSION

In all the work you are doing, work the best you can. Work as if you were doing it for the Lord, not for people.

Colossians 3:23 NCV

I have seen that there is nothing better than for a person to enjoy his activities, because that is his reward. For who can enable him to see what will happen after he dies?

Ecclesiastes 3:22 HCSB

Do not lack diligence; be fervent in spirit; serve the Lord.

Romans 12:11 HCSB

Souls who follow their hearts thrive; fools bent on evil despise matters of soul.

Proverbs 13:19 MSG

He did it with all his heart. So he prospered.

2 Chronicles 31:21 NKJV

We have every reason to be enthusiastic about life, but sometimes the struggles of daily living may cause us to feel decidedly unenthusiastic. Whenever we feel our energies begin to fade, it's time to slow down, to rest, to count our blessings, and to have a sensible talk with God. When we feel worried or weary, a few moments spent in quiet conversation with the Creator can calm our fears and restore our perspective.

Mary Lou Retton observed, "Heat is required to forge anything. Every great accomplishment is the story of a flaming heart." Is your heart aflame? Are you fully engaged in life—and in love? If so, keep up the good work! But if you feel the passion slowly draining from your life, it's time to refocus your thoughts, your energies, and your prayers . . . now.

Dear Lord, the life that I live and the words that I speak bear testimony to my faith. Make me a faithful and passionate servant of Your Son, and let my testimony be worthy of You. Let my words be sure and true, Lord, and let my actions point others to You. Amen

PATIENCE

Be completely humble and gentle; be patient, bearing with one another in love.

Ephesians 4:2 NIV

Wherefore seeing we also are compassed about with so great a cloud of witnesses, let us lay aside every weight, and the sin which doth so easily beset us, and let us run with patience the race that is set before us . . . .

Hebrews 12:1 KJV

Yet the LORD longs to be gracious to you; he rises to show you compassion. For the LORD is a God of justice. Blessed are all who wait for him!

Isaiah 30:18 NIV

Wait on the LORD; Be of good courage, and He shall strengthen your heart; Wait, I say, on the LORD!

Psalm 27:14 NKJV

We urge you, brethren, admonish the unruly, encourage the fainthearted, help the weak, be patient with everyone.

1 Thessalonians 5:14 NASB

Your students, even the most dedicated and well intentioned, are far from perfect. They make mistakes and misbehave; they don't always listen, and they don't always complete their assignments.

In an imperfect school filled with imperfect people, a teacher's patience is tested many times each day. But, God's instructions are clear: "be patient, bearing with one another in love" (Ephesians 4:2 NIV). And, that's as it should be. After all, think how patient God has been with us.

Be patient. God is using today's difficulties to strengthen you for tomorrow. He is equipping you. The God who makes things grow will help you bear fruit.

Max Lucado

Dear Lord, help me to understand the wisdom of patience. When I am hurried, slow me down. When I become impatient with others, give me empathy. Today, let me be a patient servant and a patient teacher, as I serve You and bring glory to Your Son. Amen

God's Promises About . . .

PEACE

And let the peace of God rule in your hearts . . . and be ye thankful.

Colossians 3:15 KJV

You will keep in perfect peace him whose mind is steadfast, because he trusts in you.

Isaiah 26:3 NIV

I have told you these things, so that in me you may have peace. In this world you will have trouble. But take heart! I have overcome the world.

John 16:33 NIV

The peace of God, which passeth all understanding, shall keep your hearts and minds through Christ Jesus.

Philippians 4:7 KJV

God has called us to live in peace.

1 Corinthians 7:15 NIV

As every teacher knows, peace can be a scarce commodity in a demanding, 21st-century classroom. How, then, can we find the peace that we so desperately desire? By turning our days and our lives over to God.

Jesus offers us peace, not as the world gives, but as He alone gives. We, as believers, can accept His peace or ignore it. When we accept God's peace, we are blessed; when we ignore it, we suffer bitter consequences.

Today, as a gift to yourself, to your family, and to your students, claim the inner peace that is your spiritual birthright: the peace of Jesus Christ. It is offered freely; it has been paid for in full; it is yours for the asking. So ask. And then share.

———————

Where the Spirit of the Lord is, there is peace; where the Spirit of the Lord is, there is love.

Stephen R. Adams

———————

The world talks about peace, but only You, Lord, can give a perfect and lasting peace. True peace comes through the Prince of Peace, and sometimes His peace passes all understanding. Help me to accept His peace—and share it—this day and forever. Amen

PERSEVERANCE

I do not consider myself yet to have taken hold of it. But one thing I do: Forgetting what is behind and straining toward what is ahead, I press on toward the goal to win the prize for which God has called me heavenward in Christ Jesus.

Philippians 3:13-14 NIV

Let us not become weary in doing good, for at the proper time we will reap a harvest if we do not give up.

Galatians 6:9 NIV

You need to persevere so that when you have done the will of God, you will receive what he has promised.

Hebrews 10:36 NIV

I have fought a good fight, I have finished my course, I have kept the faith.

2 Timothy 4:7 KJV

Thanks be to God! He gives us the victory through our Lord Jesus Christ. Therefore, my dear brothers, stand firm. Let nothing move you. Always give yourselves fully to the work of the Lord, because you know that your labor in the Lord is not in vain.

1 Corinthians 15:57-58 NIV

The familiar saying is true: "Life is a marathon, not a sprint." And, the same can be said of the teaching profession. Teaching requires determination, especially on those difficult days when the students are in an uproar and the lesson plan is in disarray.

In a world filled with roadblocks and stumbling blocks, we need strength, courage, and perseverance. And, as an example of perfect perseverance, we need look no further than our Savior, Jesus Christ. Our Savior finished what He began, and so must we.

Perhaps you are in a hurry for God to reveal His unfolding plans for your life. If so, be forewarned: God operates on His own timetable, not yours. Sometimes, God may answer your prayers with silence, and when He does, you must patiently persevere. In times of trouble, you must remain steadfast and trust in the merciful goodness of your Heavenly Father. Whatever your challenge, God can handle it. Your job is to keep persevering until He does.

———

If things don't work out at first, don't quit. If you never try, you'll never know how good you can be.

PRAYER

The effective prayer of a righteous man can accomplish much.

James 5:16 NASB

Whatever you ask for in prayer, believe that you have received it, and it will be yours.

Mark 11:24 NIV

I sought the LORD, and he heard me, and delivered me from all my fears.

Psalm 34:4 KJV

Ask and it shall be given to you; seek and you shall find; knock and it shall be opened to you. For every one who asks receives, and he who seeks finds, and to him who knocks it shall be opened.

Matthew 7:7-8 NASB

Rejoice evermore. Pray without ceasing. In every thing give thanks: for this is the will of God in Christ Jesus concerning you.

1 Thessalonians 5:16-18 KJV

The power of prayer: these words are so familiar, yet sometimes we forget what they mean. Prayer is a powerful tool for communicating with our Creator; it is an opportunity to commune with the Giver of all things good. Prayer helps us find strength for today and hope for the future. Prayer is a tool we can use to help others. Prayer is not a thing to be taken lightly or to be used infrequently.

Is prayer an integral part of your life, or is it a hit-or-miss habit? Do you "pray without ceasing," or is your prayer life an afterthought? Do you regularly pray for your family, your friends, and your students . . . or do you bow your head only when others are watching?

The quality of your spiritual life will be in direct proportion to the quality of your prayer life. Prayer changes things, and it changes you. Today, instead of turning things over in your mind, turn them over to God in prayer. Instead of worrying about your next decision, ask God to lead the way. Don't limit your prayers to meals or to bedtime. Pray constantly about things great and small. God is listening, and He wants to hear from you now.

Dear Lord, make me a person whose constant prayers are pleasing to You. Let me come to You often with concerns both great and small. And, when You answer my prayers, Father, let me trust Your answers, today and forever. Amen

PURPOSE

We know that all things work together for the good of those who love God: those who are called according to His purpose.

Romans 8:28 HCSB

I will instruct you and show you the way to go; with My eye on you, I will give counsel.

Psalm 32:8 HCSB

You reveal the path of life to me; in Your presence is abundant joy; in Your right hand are eternal pleasures.

Psalm 16:11 HCSB

Commit your activities to the Lord and your plans will be achieved.

Proverbs 16:3 HCSB

For it is God who is working among you both the willing and the working for His good purpose.

Philippians 2:13 HCSB

Whether you realize it or not, you are on a personal mission for God. As a Christian teacher, that mission is straightforward: Honor your Creator, accept Christ as your Savior, teach your students truth, and serve those who cross your path.

Of course, you will encounter impediments as you attempt to discover the exact nature of God's purpose for your life, but you must never lose sight of the overriding purposes that God has established for all believers through the revelations of His Holy Word. When you apply God's commandments to every aspect of your life, you will earn countless blessings for yourself, your family, and your students.

Every day offers fresh opportunities to serve God, to worship Him, and to seek His will. When you do, He will bless you in miraculous ways. May you continue to seek God's purposes, may you trust His Word, and may you place Him where He belongs: at the very center of your life.

Lord, You've got something You want me to do—help me to figure out exactly what it is. Give me Your blessings and lead me along a path that is pleasing to You . . . today, tomorrow, and forever. Amen

God's Promises About . . .

SELF-DISCIPLINE

I discipline my body and bring it under strict control, so that after preaching to others, I myself will not be disqualified.

1 Corinthians 9:27 HCSB

So prepare your minds for service and have self-control.

1 Peter 1:13 NCV

Discipline yourself for the purpose of godliness.

1 Timothy 4:7 NASB

So don't lose a minute in building on what you've been given, complementing your basic faith with good character, spiritual understanding, alert discipline, passionate patience, reverent wonder, warm friendliness, and generous love, each dimension fitting into and developing the others.

2 Peter 1:5-7 MSG

Do you not know that those who run in a race all run, but only one receives the prize? Run in such a way that you may win. Everyone who competes in the games exercises self-control in all things.

1 Corinthians 9:24-25 NASB

As leaders of the classroom, we are charged with teaching discipline and, on occasion, dispensing it. We do so in the hopes that our students will learn that disciplined behavior is at the very foundation of successful living.

Those who study the Bible are confronted again and again with God's intention that His children (of all ages) lead disciplined lives. God doesn't reward laziness or misbehavior. To the contrary, He expects His own to adopt a disciplined approach to their lives, and He punishes those who disobey His commandments.

Wise teachers demonstrate the importance of self-discipline by their words and by their actions. Wise students pay attention . . . and learn.

Simply stated, self-discipline is obedience to God's Word and willingness to submit everything in life to His will, for His ultimate glory.

John MacArthur

Dear God, today I will slow down and think about things before I do them. And when I slow down to think about things, I will always try to do what's right. Amen

SPEECH

For the one who wants to love life and to see good days must keep his tongue from evil and his lips from speaking deceit.

1 Peter 3:10 HCSB

Avoid irreverent, empty speech, for this will produce an even greater measure of godlessness.

2 Timothy 2:16 HCSB

No rotten talk should come from your mouth, but only what is good for the building up of someone in need, in order to give grace to those who hear.

Ephesians 4:29 HCSB

If anyone thinks he is religious, without controlling his tongue but deceiving his heart, his religion is useless.

James 1:26 HCSB

Pleasant words are a honeycomb: sweet to the taste and health to the body.

Proverbs 16:24 HCSB

The Bible reminds us that "Reckless words pierce like a sword, but the tongue of the wise brings healing" (Proverbs 12:18 NIV). In other words, if we are to solve more problems than we start, we must measure our words carefully.

Sometimes, even the most thoughtful teachers may speak first and think second (with decidedly mixed results). A far better strategy, of course, is to do the more difficult thing: to think first and to speak next.

Do you seek to be a source of encouragement to your students? If so, you must speak words that are worthy of your Savior. So avoid angry outbursts. Refrain from impulsive outpourings. Terminate tantrums. Instead, speak words of encouragement and hope to a world that desperately needs both.

Dear Lord, You have commanded me to choose my words carefully so that I might be a source of encouragement to my students. Keep me mindful, Lord, of the influence I have on many people. Let the words that I speak today be worthy of the One who has saved me forever. Amen

God's Promises About . . .

SPIRITUAL GROWTH

*So let us stop going over the basics of Christianity again and again.
Let us go on instead and become mature in our understanding.*

Hebrews 6:1 NLT

*Run away from infantile indulgence. Run after mature
righteousness—faith, love, peace—joining those who are in honest
and serious prayer before God.*

2 Timothy 2:22 MSG

*Know the love of Christ which surpasses knowledge, that you may
be filled up to all the fullness of God.*

Ephesians 3:19 NASB

*For this reason we also, since the day we heard it, do not cease to
pray for you, and to ask that you may be filled with the knowledge
of His will in all wisdom and spiritual understanding.*

Colossians 1:9 NKJV

Your relationship with God is ongoing; it unfolds day by day, and it offers countless opportunities to grow closer to Him . . . or not. As each new day unfolds, you are confronted with a wide range of decisions: how you will behave, where you will direct your thoughts, with whom you will associate, and what you will choose to worship. These choices, along with many others like them, are yours and yours alone. How you choose determines how your relationship with God will unfold.

Are you continuing to grow in your love and knowledge of the Lord, or are you "satisfied" with the current state of your spiritual health? Hopefully, you're determined to make yourself a growing Christian. Your Savior deserves no less, and neither, by the way, do you.

Spiritual growth consists most in the growth of the root, which is out of sight.

Matthew Henry

Lord, help me to keep growing spiritually and emotionally. Let me live according to Your Word, and let me grow in my faith every day that I live. Amen

TEACHING

Whoever gives heed to instruction prospers, and blessed is he that trusts in the Lord.

Proverbs 16:20 NIV

A wise person gets known for insight; gracious words add to one's reputation. True intelligence is a spring of fresh water, while fools sweat it out the hard way.

Proverbs 16:21-22 MSG

Simpletons only learn the hard way, but the wise learn by listening.

Proverbs 21:11 MSG

It takes wisdom to build a house, and understanding to set it on a firm foundation; it takes knowledge to furnish its rooms with fine furniture and beautiful draperies.

Proverbs 24:3-4 MSG

A wise man's heart guides his mouth, and his lips promote instruction.

Proverbs 16:23 NIV

Daniel Webster wrote, "If we work in marble, it will perish; if we work upon brass, time will efface it; if we rear temples, they will crumble into dust; but if we work upon immortal minds and instill in them just principles, we are then engraving upon tablets which no time will efface, but which will brighten and brighten to all eternity." These words remind us of the glorious opportunities that are available to those of us who teach. May we, with God's help, touch the hearts and minds of our students and, in doing so, refashion this wonderful world . . . and the next.

No teacher should strive to make men think as he thinks, but to lead them to the living Truth, to the Master Himself, of whom alone they can learn anything.

George MacDonald

Dear Lord, make me a worthy teacher, a humble servant, and a faithful disciple of Your Son Jesus. Let me guide my students in the way that You would have them go, and let me be an example of righteousness and faithfulness today and every day. Amen

God's Promises About . . .

THANKSGIVING

I will give You thanks with all my heart.

Psalm 138:1 HCSB

And whatever you do, in word or in deed, do everything in the name of the Lord Jesus, giving thanks to God the Father through Him.

Colossians 3:17 HCSB

Therefore as you have received Christ Jesus the Lord, walk in Him, rooted and built up in Him and established in the faith, just as you were taught, and overflowing with thankfulness.

Colossians 2:6-7 HCSB

Thanks be to God for His indescribable gift.

2 Corinthians 9:15 HCSB

Give thanks to the Lord, for He is good; His faithful love endures forever.

Psalm 118:29 HCSB

As believing Christians, we are blessed beyond measure. God sent His only Son to die for our sins. And, by His grace, God has given us the priceless gifts of eternal love and eternal life. We, in turn, are instructed to approach our Heavenly Father with reverence and thanksgiving. But, as busy professionals caught between the rush of everyday living and the demands of the classroom, we may sometimes fail to pause and thank our Creator for His countless blessings.

When we slow down and express our gratitude to the One who made us, we enrich our own lives and the lives of those around us. Thanksgiving should become a habit, a regular part of our daily routines. Yes, God has blessed us beyond measure, and we owe Him everything, including our eternal praise.

The act of thanksgiving is a demonstration of the fact that you are going to trust and believe God.

Kay Arthur

Dear Lord, sometimes, amid the demands of the day, I lose perspective, and I fail to give thanks for Your blessings and for Your love. Today, help me to count those blessings, and let me give thanks to You, Father, for Your love, for Your grace, for Your blessings, and for Your Son. Amen

THE JOY OF TEACHING

Be gentle to all, able to teach, patient.

2 Timothy 2:24 NKJV

Rejoice in the Lord always. I will say it again: Rejoice!

Philippians 4:4 HCSB

Light shines on the godly, and joy on those who do right. May all who are godly be happy in the Lord and praise his holy name.

Psalm 97:11-12 NLT

Celebrate God all day, every day. I mean, revel in him!

Philippians 4:4 MSG

Teach a youth about the way he should go; even when he is old he will not depart from it.

Proverbs 22:6 HCSB

Whether you teach graduate school or Sunday School, whether you lecture at seminary or at Vacation Bible School, it's important to realize that God takes your teaching duties very seriously—and so should you. After all, you are God's emissary, a person charged with molding lives—it's a truly awesome responsibility.

So, if you are fortunate enough to find yourself in the role of teacher, do yourself (and your students) a favor: celebrate the joys of your profession. Remember that God honors your contribution just as surely as He offers His loving abundance to you and your students. And with God's help, you are destined to reshape eternity. It's a big job—and you deserve to enjoy it.

Better to instruct a child than to collect riches.

Herve of Brittany

Dear Lord, today I will celebrate the joys of teaching. Help me be a cheerful, optimistic, encouraging teacher, today and every day. Amen

God's Promises About . . .

THOUGHTS

Come near to God, and God will come near to you. You sinners, clean sin out of your lives. You who are trying to follow God and the world at the same time, make your thinking pure.

James 4:8 NCV

Those who are pure in their thinking are happy, because they will be with God.

Matthew 5:8 NCV

And now, dear brothers and sisters, let me say one more thing as I close this letter. Fix your thoughts on what is true and honorable and right. Think about things that are pure and lovely and admirable. Think about things that are excellent and worthy of praise.

Philippians 4:8 NLT

Dear friend, guard Clear Thinking and Common Sense with your life; don't for a minute lose sight of them. They'll keep your soul alive and well, they'll keep you fit and attractive.

Proverbs 3:21-22 MSG

So prepare your minds for service and have self-control.

1 Peter 1:13 NCV

Our thoughts have the power to lift us up or drag us down; they have the power to energize us or deplete us, to inspire us to greater accomplishments or to make those accomplishments impossible.

God intends that you experience joy and abundance, but He will not impose His joy upon you; you must accept it for yourself. It's up to you to celebrate the life that God has given you by focusing your mind upon "whatever is of good repute" (Philippians 4:8). Today, spend more time thinking about God's blessings, and less time fretting about the minor inconveniences of life. Then, take time to thank the Giver of all things good for gifts that are glorious, miraculous, and eternal.

No matter how little we can change about our circumstances, we always have a choice about our attitude toward the situation.

Vonette Bright

Dear Lord, help me think about things that are good, things that are true, and things that are right . . . starting right now! Amen

TODAY

For he says, "In the time of my favor I heard you, and in the day of salvation I helped you." I tell you, now is the time of God's favor, now is the day of salvation.

2 Corinthians 6:2 NIV

Encourage one another daily, as long as it is Today . . . .

Hebrews 3:13 NIV

Give your entire attention to what God is doing right now, and don't get worked up about what may or may not happen tomorrow. God will help you deal with whatever hard things come up when the time comes.

Matthew 6:33-34 MSG

This is the day which the LORD has made; let us rejoice and be glad in it.

Psalm 118:24 NASB

While it is daytime, we must continue doing the work of the One who sent me. Night is coming, when no one can work.

John 9:4 NCV

The familiar words of Psalm 118 remind us that today, like every day, is a priceless gift from God. And as teachers, we are doubly blessed: we can celebrate the glory of God's creation and we can celebrate the precious students that He has entrusted to our care.

What do you expect from the day ahead? Are you expecting God to do wonderful things, or are you living beneath a cloud of apprehension and doubt? Do you expect God to use you in unexpected ways, or do you expect another uneventful day to pass with little fanfare? As a thoughtful believer, the answer to these questions should be obvious.

For Christian believers, every new day offers exciting possibilities. God's Word promises that Christ has come to this earth to give us abundant life and eternal salvation. We, in turn, should respond to God's gifts by treasuring each day and using our time here on earth to glorify our Creator and share the Good News of His Son.

Each day is a special gift from God, a treasure to be savored and celebrated. May we never fail to praise our Creator by rejoicing in His glorious creation.

Lord, You have given me another day of life; let me celebrate this day, and let me use it according to Your plan. I praise You, Father, for my life and for the friends, family, and students who make it rich. Enable me to live each moment to the fullest as I give thanks for Your love and for Your Son. Amen

WISDOM

But if any of you lacks wisdom, let him ask of God, who gives to all generously and without reproach, and it will be given to him.

James 1:5 NASB

The wisdom that is from above is first pure, then peaceable, gentle, and easy to be entreated, full of mercy and good fruits, without partiality, and without hypocrisy.

James 3:17 KJV

Reverence for the Lord is the foundation of true wisdom. The rewards of wisdom come to all who obey him.

Psalm 111:10 NLT

I will instruct you and teach you in the way you should go; I will counsel you and watch over you.

Psalm 32:8 NIV

Do not deceive yourselves. If any one of you thinks he is wise by the standards of this age, he should become a "fool" so that he may become wise. For the wisdom of this world is foolishness in God's sight.

1 Corinthians 3:18-19 NIV

Wisdom is not accumulated overnight. It is like a savings account that accrues slowly over time, and the person who consistently adds to his account will eventually accumulate a great sum. The secret to success is consistency. Do you seek wisdom for yourself and for your students? Then keep learning and keep motivating them to do likewise. The ultimate source of wisdom, of course, is—first and foremost—the Word of God. When you begin a daily study of God's Word and live according to His commandments, you will become wise . . . and so, in time, will your students.

———

Wisdom always waits for the right time to act, while emotion always pushes for action right now.

Joyce Meyer

———

Lord, make me a teacher of wisdom and discernment. Lead me in Your ways and teach me from Your Word so that, in time, my wisdom might glorify Your kingdom and Your Son. Amen

God's Promises About . . .

WORK

But as for you, be strong and do not give up, for your work will be rewarded.

2 Chronicles 15:7 NIV

Now this I say, he who sows sparingly will also reap sparingly, and he who sows bountifully will also reap bountifully.

2 Corinthians 9:6 NASB

Whatever you do, work at it with all your heart, as working for the Lord, not for men.

Colossians 3:23 NIV

Don't work hard only when your master is watching and then shirk when he isn't looking; work hard and with gladness all the time, as though working for Christ, doing the will of God with all your hearts.

Ephesians 6:6-7 TLB

Be strong and courageous, and do the work. Do not be afraid or discouraged, for the Lord God, my God, is with you.

1 Chronicles 28:20 NIV

Being a teacher is not an easy job. The demands and pressures of the classroom, combined with late-night paper-grading marathons and lesson preparations, can leave even the most experienced teacher feeling overworked and under appreciated. Thankfully, teaching is not only a difficult job; it is also a highly rewarding one.

As a teacher, you have countless opportunities to do great things for God. So it's no surprise that the teaching profession is sometimes difficult. Reaching for great things usually requires work and lots of it, which is perfectly fine with God. After all, He knows that you're up to the task, and He has big plans for you and for your students. Very big plans . . .

———————

God does not want us to work for Him, nor does He want to be our helper. Rather, He wants to do His work in and through us.

Vonette Bright

———————

Dear Lord, make my work pleasing to You. Help me to sow the seeds of Your abundance in the classroom and everywhere I go. Let me be diligent in all my undertakings and give me patience to wait for Your harvest. Amen

God's Promises About . . .

WORRY

Don't worry about anything, but in everything, through prayer and petition with thanksgiving, let your requests be made known to God.

Philippians 4:6 HCSB

Therefore don't worry about tomorrow, because tomorrow will worry about itself. Each day has enough trouble of its own.

Matthew 6:34 HCSB

Yea, though I walk through the valley of the shadow of death, I will fear no evil: for thou art with me; thy rod and thy staff they comfort me.

Psalm 23:4 KJV

I will be with you when you pass through the waters . . . when you walk through the fire . . . the flame will not burn you. For I the Lord your God, the Holy One of Israel, and your Savior.

Isaiah 43:2-3 HCSB

Don't worry about your life, what you will eat or what you will drink; or about your body, what you will wear. Isn't life more than food and the body more than clothing?

Matthew 6:25 HCSB

Because we are imperfect human beings, we worry. Even though we, as Christians, have the assurance of salvation—even though we, as Christians, have the promise of God's love and protection—we find ourselves fretting over the countless details of everyday life.

Perhaps you are concerned about the inevitable changes of everyday life. Perhaps you are uncertain about your future or your finances. Or perhaps you are simply a "worrier" by nature. If so, take your worries to God. Remember that your loving Creator sits in heaven and you are His beloved child. And as you ponder upon these facts, perhaps, you will worry a little less and trust God a little more, and you are protected with God's love.

The very essence of anxious care is imagining that we are wiser than God. When we worry, we put ourselves in his place and try to do for him what he intends to do for us.

C. H. Spurgeon

When I worship You, Lord, You direct my path and You cleanse my heart. Let today and every day be a time of worship and praise. Let me worship You in everything that I think and do. Thank You, Lord, for the priceless gift of Your Son Jesus. Let me be worthy of that gift, and let me give You the praise and the glory forever. Amen

God's Promises About . . .

WORSHIP

Then saith Jesus unto him, Get thee hence, Satan: for it is written, Thou shalt worship the Lord thy God, and him only shalt thou serve.

Matthew 4:10 KJV

Blessed are they which do hunger and thirst after righteousness: for they shall be filled.

Matthew 5:6 KJV

Worship the Lord with gladness. Come before him, singing with joy. Acknowledge that the Lord is God! He made us, and we are his. We are his people, the sheep of his pasture.

Psalm 100:2-3 NLT

Happy are those who hear the joyful call to worship, for they will walk in the light of your presence, Lord.

Psalm 89:15 NLT

But the hour cometh, and now is, when the true worshippers shall worship the Father in spirit and in truth: for the Father seeketh such to worship him.

John 4:23 KJV

We should never deceive ourselves: every life is based upon some form of worship. The question is not whether we worship, but what we worship.

Some of us choose to worship God. The result is a plentiful harvest of joy, peace, and abundance. Others distance themselves from God by foolishly worshiping earthly possessions and personal gratification. To do so is a mistake of profound proportions.

Have you accepted the grace of God's only begotten Son? Then worship Him. Worship Him today and every day. Worship Him with sincerity and thanksgiving. Write His name on your heart and rest assured that He, too, has written your name on His.

To worship is to quicken the conscience by the holiness of God, to feed the mind with the truth of God, to open the heart to the love of God, to devote the will to the purpose of God.

William Temple

Heavenly Father, let today and every day be a time of worship. Let me worship You, not only with words and deeds, but also with my heart. In the quiet moments of the day, let me praise You and thank You for creating me, loving me, guiding me, and saving me. Amen